Protest and the State in Eurasia and West Asia

Protest and the State in Eurasia and West Asia

Edited by

Priya Singh

Anita Sengupta

Suchandana Chatterjee

Maulana Abul Kalam Azad Institute of Asian Studies
Kolkata

in association with

KNOWLEDGE WORLD

KW Publishers Pvt Ltd
New Delhi

The **Maulana Abul Kalam Azad Institute of Asian Studies** (MAKAIAS) is an autonomous body under the Ministry of Culture, Government of India. Based in Kolkata, it was registered as a Society under the West Bengal Registration of Societies' Act of 1961 on the 4th of January 1993, with Prof. Nurul Hasan, the then Governor of West Bengal, as the President of the Society. It is funded by the Department of Culture, Government of India.

MAKAIAS is a centre for research and learning with a focus on social, cultural, economic and political / administrative developments in Asia from the middle of the 19th Century onwards, with special emphasis on their links with India, and also on the life and works of Maulana Abul Kalam Azad.

ISBN 978-93-83649-98-3

KNOWLEDGE WORLD

Published in India by

Kalpana Shukla
KW Publishers Pvt Ltd
4676/21, First Floor, Ansari Road, Daryaganj, New Delhi 110002
Phone: +91.11.23263498/43528107
Email: knowledgeworld@kwpub.com • www.kwpub.com

2011 FPBA BEST PUBLISHERS AWARD (ENGLISH)

Printed and Bound by Bhavish Graphics.

Contents

Movements and Counter-Movements

Contributors

Claude Arpi, Author, Columnist and Tibetologist. He can be contacted at claudearpi@gmail.com. He blogs at http://claudearpi.blogspot.com/

Kamoluddin Abdullaev, Policy analyst and independent conflict resolution consultant. He can be contacted at kamolkhon@yahoo.com; Personal webpage: kamolkhon.com.

Aidar Amrebayev, Head of the Institute for World Economy and Politics under the Foundation of First President of Kazakhstan. He can be contacted at aidar.amrebayev@gmail.com.

Aigul Akhanova, She can be contacted at 2014aigul7@gmail.com.

Olga Malinova, Chief Research Fellow of the Institute of Scientific Information for Social Sciences, Russian Academy of Sciences and Professor of Political Science, Department of the Moscow Institute of International Relations (University). Also Professor, Department of Applied Political Science of the Higher School of Economics. She can be contacted at omalinova@mail.ru.

Anita Sengupta, Former Fellow, Maulana Abul Kalam Azad Institute of Asian Studies. She can be contacted at anitasengupta@hotmail.com.

Tamar Hermann, Professor of Political Science and Dean of Academic Studies at the Open University (OU) of Israel. She also serves as a Senior Research Fellow at the Israel Democracy Institute and a co-director of the Peace Index project at Tel Aviv University. She can be contacted at tamarhe@gmail.com.

Zeev Rosenhek, Associate Professor at the Department of Sociology, Political Science and Communication at the Open University of Israel. He can be contacted at zeev.rosenhek@gmail.com.

Michael Shalev, Professor at the Department of Sociology, Anthropology and Political Science, Hebrew University, Jerusalem. He can be contacted at michael.shalev@gmail.com.

Fatemeh Sadeghi, Tehran-based Researcher of Political Thought and Women's Studies and a member of the Editorial Board of the journal *Goft-o-Gu*. She can be contacted at sadeghif@gmail.com.

Ranjit Gupta, Retired Indian Foreign Service officer; Distinguished Fellow at Institute of Peace and Conflict Studies (IPCS), New Delhi. He can be contacted at ranjit100@gmail.com.

Introduction

The twenty-first century has been witness to disaffection and protest across Eurasia and West Asia, bringing into question the state of governance as also a redefinition of the arc of crisis. A large part of the discussion is polarised between those who focus on the absence of governance/failed states and others who emphasise technology induced political mobilisation as the primary motivating factor for the protests. While the Arab Spring is widely recognised as the culmination of the series of protests and "colour revolutions" across Eurasia and West Asia, reverberations have continued with the Maidan in Ukraine and sporadic protests in Turkey. The trigger has been issues as varied as climate change and subsequent drought or water scarcity, economic inequalities impelled by a globalisation process which caters to certain sections of society, social grievances of marginalised sections who feel politically, socially or culturally betrayed by the state and a general failure to address critical issues in a timely manner.

The Arab Spring has garnered ample attention for the Arab World. The image of the Arab Spring that has endured in the popular imagination is one in which a wave of mass mobilisation swept across West Asia, ousted autocrats, and paved the way for democracy. The truth is that a small number of Arab countries have experienced anything of the nature, and only a handful of the fourteen Arab countries witnessed regime change. It is imperative to look into the full range of variance: from the lack or failure of uprisings in nations such as Algeria and Saudi Arabia on the one hand, to Tunisia's unsteady but still encouraging transition on the other. The haphazard manner in which protests spread implied that a wide range of regimes faced popular protests. The grievances of protesters seized attention because the demonstrations of the Arab Spring were the most convincing articulation of popular discontent that these countries had witnessed in years. The pace with which previously dissimilar social groups succeeded in organising collectively to challenge regimes unsurprisingly lured analysts to focus on the new information technologies that apparently made such collective action conceivable.

However the chronicle of youthful daring and technological savoir-faire goes only thus far. Protesters across the region had access to Twitter, Facebook, and YouTube, and yet the reality of most democratic activists in the Arab world remains one of disillusionment and failure.

While most debates on the upheaval against absolutism and suppression, encompassed explications such as the social media, youth unemployment and citizens' protest to redeem self-esteem in societies humiliated by unjust regimes, these can only illuminate some symptoms of a social problem, while leaving unexplained the economic and political structures that contributed to it. Some notable outcomes of quiescence, resource-based ethnic and sectarian conflicts and a faulty development paradigm are deepened inequality and a wedge between the victors and the vanquished, or prosperity, fortune and influence in contrast to poverty and deprivation among the condemned, unemployed and desperate multitude. To complement prevalent explanations of the Arab Spring as a youth revolt aided by social media in a globally networked society, there is a need to engage in other key aspects of the protests against the state along with its ramifications and responses from the centre.

In Eurasia, the moment of protest arrived with the onset of *glasnost* and *perestroika*. The euphoria of reform culminated in pluralist voices that reverberated in the Baltics and Central Asia. Popular Front organisations in Central Asia like *Birlik* and *Erk* agitated for greater autonomy in economic and cultural issues. Kazakhstan's *Zheltoqsan* uprising of 1986 is a source of pride among ethnic Kazakhs who view it as the first public demonstration of local sentiments. Aspirations of independence were strongest in the Baltic region. Collective political behaviour became the norm for the mass movements that swept across the Baltic republics. Similarly, debates continue around the March 2005 Tulip Revolution, with opinion divided between those who consider the significance of the events in terms of a change of regime and constitutional reform through a national referendum and others who see the continuation of the revolution till a number of issues, including corruption, are resolved. There have been echoes of such protests two decades later in Ukraine's Maidan. Of a completely different character are protest movements in Tibet, Xinjiang and Inner Mongolia that are usually typecast as China's problem and have evoked sharp global responses. Voices of exit are not uncommon in the Caucasus or the western and eastern fringes of Asiatic Russia.

Over the years, there have been variations of protest in Central Asia—"violent protest" (discussed widely as ethno-nationalist and intra-regional/*mahalgaroi*) perceived as the logical culmination of Soviet "order" that created disaffection among regions within the Soviet space and also due to the proliferation of patronage networks. The range of protest varied from ethno-nationalist protest to regionalist demands and economic grievances in an era of transition to market economy. Russia became the scene of protest immediately after the 1991 August coup which saw the disintegration of the USSR. Moscow became associated with anti-coup protest movements though demonstrations in large numbers actually took place in cities like Leningrad, Nizhni Novgorod, Saratov, Tomsk and Vladivostok where protests, though extensive, were not aimed at overthrowing the Yeltsin regime. During Putin's first term in the 2000s, new protests focused on specific issues like devaluation of the rouble, "reforms" initiated by Yevgeny Primakov and rising oil prices, emerged. During Putin's second term, the protests against the regime escalated in the regions of Russia, especially in the provincial centres. The content of protest changed as satire and humour ridiculing Russian Presidency assumed importance. Regime change has become an issue among protesters in Russia today.

The need to reflect on moments of protest has increasingly gained importance. There is need to further analyse the role of the international community in what is often identified as matters of domestic concern and the acceptability of intervention in situations where protest leads to conflict. While the nature of the protests has been as diverse as the reaction of authorities to the protest, there has been a tendency to review the replication of the protests across states in the region. This brings to the forefront a number of issues including the specificity of protests across Eurasia and West Asia, the level of popular involvement, the role of the social media in the protests, symbols and images of the protests and extent to which engagement with the global community allow for greater scope for debate and protest.

With a view to engaging in at least some of the afore-mentioned issues, the Maulana Abul Kalam Azad Institute of Asian Studies organised an international seminar, entitled *Protest and the State in Eurasia and West Asia* in November 2014. In a broad sense the seminar sought to analyse the relations between the state and protests wherein its aim was to explore the construction of protest movements delving into the background, nature and specificity of dissent. Another aspect that the debates intended to understand and interpret was the moments and episodes associated with movements, capturing, disseminating and transmuting the images and symbols of protest. The idea was to examine and discuss protest movements and counter-movements. The world is increasingly observing and partaking in local and global acts of protest and solidarity that entail visual, aural, and behavioural articulations by demonstrators as effective ways of making claims, reclaim spaces, and condemn invasive situations. Protesters are employing performance methods which augment the reach and tone of the local protests as well as carry the potential of being replicated in other parts of the world, creating linkages of empathy and convergence within a larger social movement. As these contemporary multi-sited protests challenge scholars to rethink their notions of resistance, the primary concern of the academic forum was to enquire about and debate on whether contemporary protesters are consolidating on and intensifying prior repertoires of dissent.

The Construction of Protest Movements

The first cluster of essays, loosely grouped under the category of the "Construction of Protest Movements," contend with protest movements in Tibet, Tajikistan in particular and Central Asia as a whole. Claude Arpi's essay, *Evolution of Protests in Tibet (1959-2008)* examines the evolution of protests on the Tibetan plateau between 1959 and 2008. It is divided into three phases: first, the events around the 1959 "uprising" (or "rebellion," for the Chinese) and the subsequent escape of the Dalai Lama to India, an event still disturbing the Chinese leadership; second, the more localised, but highly publicised 1987-1989 unrest in the streets of Lhasa, which ended with the imposition of Martial Law in March 1989; and finally the events of March-April 2008 which spread like wildfire on the entire plateau. Arpi argues that though the three phases—separated by nearly 60 years—are different in terms of manifestation and physical location, the reasons which triggered them are the same: a deep resentment against the imposition of a foreign way of life on the Tibetan local population, a strong reaction against the presence of the Chinese People's Liberation Army (PLA) in the 1950s and lastly, the important influx of Han civilian migrants. The central question posed by the author is, "Can the circle of protests be broken?" For Arpi it is a difficult question to answer, but one worth attempting.

The next essay in this grouping is Kamoluddin Abdullaev's *The Protest Movement and Political Change in Tajikistan.* Abdullaev contends that Tajikistan has experienced one of the most difficult state-building projects among the former Soviet Republics. Since the late Soviet period the country has experienced a rapid rise in political activism, civil war and ethnic cleansings, an internationally led peace process, the integration of opposition forces into government, disarmament of former combatants, moderation of radical Islamism and their inclusion, redistribution of power amongst regions, promotion of multipartyism and freedoms and recent exclusion and dramatic slide to destabilisation and the return of authoritarianism and repression. The essay narrates how immediately after the collapse of the USSR, Tajikistan became a scene of brutal civil war, taking place in one of the global hubs of religiously motivated political struggle, militancy, mass cross-border refugee flows, insurgency, and drug trafficking. In 2000, Tajikistan with the help of the international community broke out of its cycle of violence and economic decline after ending the civil war through a negotiated settlement. The country was making modest progress toward stability. However, the heavy burden of socio-economic problems, in addition to the conflict in the neighbouring Afghanistan-Pakistan, a series of protests and "colour revolution" across Eurasia and "jihadi" challenge presented even bigger problems for Tajikistan. In a nutshell, the essay focuses on social movements in Tajikistan, beginning with the late Soviet period to the present. It discusses the social impulse for protest, considers the strategies of social movements, and looks at the institutional response to protest, and finally puts forth a query: what is the impact on the structure and development of the state on social movements itself?

The final essay in the first set is Aidar Amrebayev and Aigul Akhanova's *Water Resource Management in Central Asia: An Issue of Social Conflict.* The authors argue that although experts assert that unequal distribution of water resources and water shortage have an influence on the potential for social conflict in Central Asia, recent sources have confirmed that water wastage, excessive water demand, ineffective treaties and water management also have an influence on the economic condition of local people. Hence, economic issues have the potential to influence social conflicts in Central Asia. In this context, Amrebayev and Akhanova raise and attempt to address a couple of critical concerns such as, "Are the five states of Central Asia (Kazakhstan, Uzbekistan, Turkmenistan, Tajikistan and Kyrgyzstan) capable of solving regional water and economic issues for their common interest?" and "What is the best model of water management for Central Asian states to reduce the potential of social conflicts?"

Moments, Imaginings and Movements

The second set of essays has been grouped as reflecting "Moments, Imaginings and Movements." Olga Malinova's essay *Exploring the Symbolic Dimension of Social Protest: An Analysis of Public Representations of Opposition to Putin's Regime During the Moscow Protest Campaign of 2011-2012,* begins with a discussion of theoretical issues concerning symbolic aspects of social protest in general and in the electoral authoritarian regimes in particular, paying special attention to the effects of media and visualisation. The paper then moves on to an analysis of public representations of opposition to the Putin regime in the Moscow protest campaign, focusing on symbolic means of construction of the identity of the protesters. For the purpose of doing so, the author argues that she draws attention to the public discussions about "modernisation," the "middle class" and "corruption" that, in her opinion, contributed to self-conception of the protest movement. In the final analysis, Malinova claims that there was a decline in the protest movement after June 2012. This was facilitated by reinterpretation of its frames by its opponents in the context of Putin's re-election whereby the symbolic contestation changed significantly.

The other essay in this cluster is Anita Sengupta's *The Politics of Exclusion: Rhetoric, Symbolism and Gezi Park.* The essay plays on the assumption that rhetoric remains one of the most interesting and debated aspects of political communication and in its turn, the rhetoric that particular events generate becomes an important part of the political process. Rhetoric and symbolism are interwoven and convenient ways to reach the target as they are routinely relayed by the press. Along with symbolism and myths, rhetoric performs a key role in political communication and propaganda. Sengupta argues that while in most situations rhetoric is invoked for inclusion, in some it performs the role of exclusion and this became evident during the incidents following the Gezi Park protests when a sharp differentiation was recognised, in the political rhetoric of the leadership among followers of the AKP (*Adalet ve Kalkinma Partisi* or Justice and Development Party) and those who had opposed its policies in the course of the protests. The symbolism that Gezi Park produced was something that the political leadership found difficult to comprehend and the contradiction between qualifying the protests as "concern for a few trees" and simultaneously an "international plot" was reflective of this. The government however was not alone in the race to appropriate the symbolic value of the protests. Gezi Park also generated rhetoric from among the protesters who contributed their own subversive slogans and visual images. The Gezi Park protesters were exceedingly good at developing a discourse by using strong sense of humour, incorporating music in their power of opposition and employing the social media. The essay studies both the rhetoric of exclusion generated by the ruling establishment and the counter rhetoric generated by the protesters who, in Sengupta's opinion, in a number of cases inverted the same rhetoric to their advantage.

Protest and the State

The two essays which have been bracketed under, "Protest and the State," deal with demonstrations against the state in Israel. In *Gone with the Wind or a Tectonic Change? A Retrospective Analysis Based on the 2011 Israeli Socio-Political Protest Campaign***,** Tamar Hermann examines what she terms as "a massive socio-economic grass-roots protest," which had erupted in Israel in the summer of 2011. The initiators of this campaign, according to the author were predominantly young adults who demanded strategic changes in the government's social and economic policies, i.e., the reversal of the neoliberal economy. Their criticism focused on the high cost of living in general, and that of housing in particular, but beyond these, suggested a new approach to national priority scaling. Public opinion polls indicated overwhelming support for the campaign as well as with its operative repertoire. Even among those public sectors which were not present in large numbers in the streets, a significant level of approval was recorded. Hermann argues that scepticism appeared to have left the stage free for hope. The article examines why the 2011 Israeli social-economic protest campaign eventually dissipated. It addresses another issue, which is the balance sheet of the fulfilled and unfulfilled promises of the protest. Hermann also recommends some wide-ranging insights regarding the potential effectiveness and resilience of such campaigns in democratic regimes in a globalised world. The first part of the essay concisely presents the central theoretical approaches to the emergence of political protest campaigns. The second part describes the lifecycle of the 2011 Israeli social-economic campaign. The third part depicts its four-year-old legacies and offers certain suppositions regarding the potential of such campaigns to last and introduce significant changes in the political system.

Zeev Rosenhek and Michael Shalev's *Economic Demands and Sociocultural Identities: The "Social Justice" Protests in Israel* also contend with the protests that unexpectedly broke out in Israel in the summer of 2011 under the slogan "the people demand social justice," and, in the opinion of the authors, succeeded in dominating the public agenda for two tumultuous months. The essay analyses the connections between the socioeconomic character of the protests and processes of collective identity formation that evolved around the massive mobilisation that took place in Israel during the summer of 2011. The authors observe that making broad and inclusionary demands for a comprehensive welfare state and a more equal distribution of economic resources, the protest movement attempted to articulate an all-embracing Israeli collective identity intended to transcend the deep-seated and long-lasting sociopolitical and cultural divides characterising Israeli society. According to Rosenhek and Shalev, in its efforts to cross deeply entrenched sociocultural boundaries emerging from solidarities based on ethnicity, religiosity, lifestyle and cultural-political habitus, the protests indeed represented a remarkable novelty in Israeli politics. The essay examines the tensions between the material and cultural interests of the protest's initiators deriving from their class-generational background on the one hand and their attempt to build an inclusive identity that would rise above societal cleavages and conflicts on the other, as a key dynamics that fundamentally affected the protest's character and trajectory. Focusing on the dialectic relationship and tensions between an inclusionary formulation of membership and demands and pre-existing deep socio-political and cultural divides, the authors claim that the analysis contributes to the study of the character and dynamics of the presumably all-encompassing movements that comprise the current global wave of protest.

Movements and Counter-Movements

The final set of essays, which have been branded as pertaining to "Movements and Counter-Movements," deal with the protest movements and their repercussions in the Middle East at large and the Arab world in particular. Fatemeh Sadeghi's *Amid Empire States: Protest Movements in the Transforming Middle East* examines what the author contends has taken place in recent years, wherein the Middle Eastern states have experienced a structural transformation, from nation-state to the state of emergency. Sadeghi argues that parallel to the global trend, capital accumulation and over-accumulation paved the way for the rise of emergency states. As a result, previous nation-states seem to have gradually been replaced by emergency states whose function and aims are different from those of nation-states. Rather than governing the societies, they tend to be sovereign through policing apparatus, neoliberal and crony capitalist relations, and hegemonic expansion in space and time. This transformation in the author's opinion appears to have made profound impact on the protest movements of the Middle East, namely the Green Movement in Iran, the Gezi movement in Turkey, the Syrian uprising, Human Rights Movement of Bahrain, and Revolutionary Movements in Egypt, Tunisia, and Libya.

The final essay of the volume, Ranjit Gupta's essay, *Ruminations on the Characteristics and Consequences of Political Protests in the Arab World,* has been written from the perspective of a diplomatic practitioner. The author explicitly states that the subject is consciously not examined in a purely theoretical sense but is related to actual events and happenings that have or are taking place in the Arab world. The essay consists of a number of sections, which comprehensively deals with various aspects relating to political protests in the Arab world. Taking cognizance of the fact that the Arab world is a distinct political grouping with characteristics which distinguish it from other regional political groupings—in particular its being an island of autocracies as compared to any other group of countries in any continent—how this particular characteristic relates to and affects the nature of protests is examined. The author contends that protests in the Arab world have more frequently than not mutated into armed insurrections, and why this happens in the Arab world much more than in other socio-political groupings of countries, is a query posed and analysed in the essay. A section of the essay deals with protests in the Arab world becoming heavily infused with religion and the reasons behind this phenomenon. In this context the intellectual sources and motivation of the nature of the consequent protest are also briefly studied. Another section examines how protests in the Arab world have become transnational movements and traces the evolution and nature of the most prominent of these transnational protest groups. The trajectory of protests in a few selected countries of the Arab world is also analysed. The final section of the essay is in the nature of a prognosis for the future.

The collection of essays in this volume is an attempt at examining and providing specific insights based on the debates and discussions in a seminar, which aimed at an analysis of the various aspects of protest and resistance and their repercussions in the Eurasian and West Asian region.

The Construction of Protest Movements

1. Evolution of Protests in Tibet (1959-2008)

Claude Arpi

This paper will study the evolution of protests on the Tibetan plateau between 1959 and 2008. It is divided in 3 phases: first, the events around the 1959 "uprising" (or "rebellion," for the Chinese) and the subsequent escape of the Dalai Lama to India, an event still disturbing the Chinese leadership; second, the more localised, but highly publicised 1987-1989 unrest in the streets of Lhasa, which ended with the imposition of Martial Law in March 1989; and finally the events of March-April 2008 which spread like wildfire on the entire plateau. Though the three phases, separated by nearly 60 years, are different in terms of manifestation and physical location, the reasons which triggered them are the same: a deep resentment against the imposition of a foreign way of life on the Tibetan local population, a strong reaction against the presence of the Chinese People's Liberation Army (PLA) in the 1950s and lastly, the important influx of Han civilian migrants. Can the circle of protests be broken? It is a difficult question to answer, but one can try.

The Background

On October 7, 1950, Tibet was invaded by the People's Liberation Army (PLA). The "liberation" of Tibet was a masterly "coup" by Mao. He wanted to show the world who the real leader of Asia was, while simultaneously demonstrating that India was incapable of defending a smaller country with whom she had close cultural and historic links. On May 13, 1951, a "17-Point Agreement for the Peaceful Liberation of Tibet" was signed in Beijing between China and some Tibetan delegates. The Tibetans later asserted that it was forced on them, "under duress." For the first time in their history, they had to accept China's suzerainty; Article 1 says: "The Tibetan people shall unite and drive out imperialist aggressive forces from Tibet; the Tibetan people shall return to the big family of the Motherland—the People's Republic of China."[1]

In 1954, the nineteen-year-old Dalai Lama was keen to "understand" New China; he spent several months in Beijing and travelled through the mainland. During his stay in Beijing he had the occasion to meet the Chinese leaders (including Mao Zedong several times), and could discuss the Tibet issue. Mao and his colleagues were however adamant that Tibet needed to be "liberated," a concept that the Tibetan monk did not really understand. While returning from Beijing in 1955, the Dalai Lama's representatives visited Eastern Tibet, where unrest had broken out in several places. George Patterson, the Scottish Missionary living in Kham in the early 1950s, wrote: "In early 1956, Chamdo, Batang, Gantze and Lithang had their Chinese garrisons wiped out by marauding Khampa rebels."[2]

A few months earlier, the arrest of Lobsang Tsewong, a leader from Amdo, had triggered the revolt in this Province. According to Patterson: "This precipitated a series of local uprisings and demonstrations against the Chinese in Amdo, and the Peking Government ordered more Chinese troops into the area to subdue the area once and for all. But when a unit of Chinese troops arrived in the Golok tribal area, the Goloks captured them, disarmed them, cut off their noses and sent them back mutilated to their garrison as a contemptuous warning."[3] The Khampa rebellion was the seed of the protests which occurred in Lhasa a few years later. The imposition of so-called reforms by the Communist regime in Beijing on Central Tibet triggered the first protests.

The First Phase: 1959

In 1957-58, the situation continued to deteriorate in Central Tibet. The Tibetan population was resentful of what they considered the occupation of their country. The fact that this "colonisation" force was atheist (Mao had said to the Dalai Lama in Beijing that "religion is a poison"), made the situation worse. It culminated on March 10, 1959, when the entire population of the Tibetan capital revolted against the occupiers. The Chinese immediately retaliated by indiscriminately firing at the Tibetan crowds and bombing some buildings such as the Potala, the winter palace of the Dalai Lamas. The uprising ended after two weeks, resulting in ten thousand civilian deaths.

The Dalai Lama, speaking in the third person, later explained the background of the events of March 1959:

> The Dalai Lama had agreed a month in advance to attend a cultural show in the Chinese headquarters and the date was suddenly fixed for the 10th of March. The people of Lhasa became apprehensive that some harm might be done to the Dalai Lama and as a result about ten thousand people gathered round the Dalai Lama's summer palace, Norbulingka, and physically prevented the Dalai Lama from attending the function. Thereafter, the people themselves decided to raise a bodyguard for the protection of the Dalai Lama. Large crowds of Tibetans went about the streets of Lhasa demonstrating against the Chinese rule in Tibet. Two days later, thousands of Tibetan women held demonstrations protesting against Chinese authority. In spite of this demonstration from the people, the Dalai Lama and his government endeavoured to maintain friendly relations with the Chinese and tried to carry out negotiations with the Chinese representatives on how best to bring about peace in Tibet and assuage the people's anxiety. While these negotiations were being carried out, reinforcements arrived to strengthen the Chinese garrisons in Lhasa and Tibet.[4]

Ultimately, the Dalai Lama left Lhasa on March 17 to take refuge in India. In the *Political and Military History of Tibet*, Gyaltse Namgyal Wangdu recounts that after the Dalai Lama's departure, the Tibetans began to organise the resistance:

> Many people, old and young, ordained and lay, from different parts of the three provinces of Tibet, rushed to give food and daily necessities to the volunteers at Norbulingka and other areas of Lhasa, and the roads appeared to be filled with the heavy traffic of people. That marked an unprecedented unity of the Tibetan people of the whole of Tibet.[5]

Unfortunately, it did not last long! Wangdu continues:

> At around 2.00 a.m. on March 20, 1959, the Chinese at first fired artillery from the western side of Magar Sarpa, the new "New Regimental Headquarters," followed immediately by Kyangthang Nakha (meadow near Norbulingka) and Tsedrunglingka park. They finally started firing from within Lhasa. The Tibetan forces at Lhasa and Norbulingka made counterattacks. Amidst the intense exchange of fire between them, we could see the bright signal-lights of white, red and green colors fired into the sky from various sides.

> The whole area of Lhasa was filled with the intense noise of artillery and gunshots. The Tibetan forces at different positions gave signals to each other by trumpet to remain alert and ready to charge at the Chinese forces. Sparks of bullets and shells soared high into the sky from everywhere. Sometimes bullets and shells passed near us, with whistling sounds. Since it was dark and there were only a few electric lights at the Chinese army camps, both the Chinese and Tibetan forces fired artillery and guns at their enemy's positions, by guessing their distance and locations.[6]

This explosion of violence was unexpected and mainly due to the revolt of the "common men."

The official website of the Tibetan Government-in-Exile,[7] quoting a Radio Lhasa broadcast of October 1, 1960, affirms that some 87,000 Tibetans were killed during the days which followed the uprising and the departure of the Dalai Lama.

The First Chinese Statements

The Dalai Lama was already heading towards India when the Chinese discovered that the Dalai Lama had left his palace. They reacted violently. A communiqué issued by the *New China News Agency* in Beijing on March 28, stated: "Violating the will of the Tibetan People and betraying the motherland, the Tibetan Local Government and the upper-strata reactionary clique colluded with imperialism, assembled rebellious bandits and launched armed attacks against the PLA Garrison in Lhasa during the night of March 19. Acting on orders to put the rebellion down, the valiant units of the PLA stationed in Tibet completely smashed the rebellious bandits in the city of Lhasa on March 22. Now the units of the PLA, assisted by patriotic people of all sections, both religious and secular, are mopping up the rebellious bandits in other places in Tibet."[8]

Xinhua News Agency gave its version of the events: "The armed rebellion of the Tibetan Local Government and the reactionary clique of the upper strata in Lhasa began on March 10. The Dalai Lama had originally planned to attend a theatrical performance in the auditorium of the Tibetan Military Area Command of the People's Liberation Army on March 10. The proposal was put forth by the Dalai Lama personally more than one month earlier and the date of March 10 was fixed by the Dalai Lama himself. On that day, however, the rebellious Tibetan clique spread wild rumours alleging that the army units of the Tibetan Military Area Command would detain the Dalai Lama and, using this rumour as a pretext, staged an armed rebellion, put the Dalai Lama under duress, raised such reactionary slogans as 'Drive away the Han people' and 'Independence for Tibet.'[9]

For the first time since the Liberation Army had entered Tibet in 1950, the Chinese government admitted to disturbances in Tibet and widespread revolts against the Chinese occupants. It was something new for Mao. During the days of the Long March, the Great Helmsman had always been welcomed as a hero by the Chinese masses; wherever the Liberation Army went, the ordinary people received them as liberators and provided food and logistic support. It was in Tibet that for the first the time, the masses did not accept the "liberation" forces. Though the Communist propaganda continued to explain that it was only a serfs' rebellion against the upper strata "Dalai's clique" and that only the clergy and the aristocracy were involved in the uprising, it is a fact that the March 10 was a movement of the "masses" who were ready to give their lives to defend their leader.

In India: In the Lok Sabha

The uprising was mentioned for the first time in the Lok Sabha on March 23, 1959, when Prime Minister Jawaharlal Nehru made a statement. At that time, news was sparse as the only channel of communication was the Indian Consul General in Lhasa through wireless. Nehru informed the house: "We have since received fuller information from our Consul General in Lhasa.[10] It appears that various rumours in regard to the Dalai Lama caused excitement in Lhasa. About two weeks ago, a large crowd of Tibetans entered the premises of the Indian Consulate General. They spoke to our Consul General about the rumours and their apprehensions."[11]

The Prime Minister continued to give a report of the situation in Lhasa:

> Three days later, a large number of Tibetan women came to our Consulate General and requested our Consul General to accompany them to the Chinese Foreign Bureau and be a witness to their presenting certain demands. … On March 20, fighting suddenly broke out between the Chinese troops and Tibetan elements. There was firing in the vicinity of our Consulate General and some stray bullets hit our building. For some time it was not possible for the Consul General to go out of the premises. All our staff and their families are safe and no significant damage to property has

> been reported. Apparently, the situation in Lhasa has somewhat quietened down.[12]

This marks the end of the first phase. Incidentally, China today celebrates March 28 as the Serf Emancipation Day; it is the day they regained control over Lhasa. In Chinese words:

> The rebellious activities of the Tibetan traitors have been of fairly long duration. These rebels represent imperialism and the most reactionary major serf owners. ... But as the motherland is thriving and prospering day by day, the policy of the Central People's Government toward Tibet is correct, and the garrison units of the People's Liberation Army in Tibet observe strict discipline, all enjoy the warm support and love of the people of all sections in Tibet and the rebellious conspiracy of a handful of reactionaries had no support from the Tibetan people.[13]

In 2009, the Tibetan regional parliament passed a bill approving the celebrations of March 28 as the date as the Serf Emancipation Day. It marks, according to Beijing, the date when one million people were freed from serfdom and it reminds "all the Chinese people, including Tibetans, of the landmark democratic reform initiated 50 years ago." This was Beijing's point of view. The most interesting aspect of the 1959 Uprising/Rebellion was that it was a mass movement followed by the entire population of Lhasa. It was not, as Beijing later pretended, an incident triggered by an upper-strata clique or a few reactionaries.

The Second Phase: 1987-1989

As far as the participation of the Tibetan population is concerned, the second phase between 1987 and 1989 was more limited. This time, the protests, at the beginning at least, were led mainly by monks of the three large monasteries around Lhasa. Geographically, it was also limited to Lhasa and its surroundings. It began in Washington DC on September 21, 1987, when the Dalai Lama addressed the members of the US Congressional Human Rights' Caucus. He presented his "Five Point Peace Plan for Tibet." The Plan was well received not only in the United States, but also in Europe. Many saw the new proposals as a positive step towards solving the Tibetan issue and for durable peace in Asia.

The Five Points asked for "democratic reforms" and requested early negotiations:

- Transformation of the whole Tibet into a zone of peace.
- Abandonment by China of its population transfer policy which threatens the very existence of the Tibetans as a race.
- Respect of the Tibetan people's fundamental rights and democratic reforms.
- Restoration and protection of Tibet's natural environment and abandonment of China's use of Tibet for the production of nuclear weapons and dumping of nuclear waste.
- Commencement of earnest negotiations on the future status of Tibet and of the relations between the people of Tibet and China.[14]

Six days after the Dalai Lama had announced his Plan in Washington, the first demonstration erupted in Lhasa. This eventually degenerated into a series of riots, the worst since 1959, and finally the clamping down of martial law in March 1989. As in 1959, the protests were restricted to Lhasa. Unrest continued sporadically during the following two years. One of the reasons was that a hardliner, Hu Jintao,[15] had been nominated Party Chief for Tibet. During the following years, the Chinese learned their lesson; surveillance with sophisticated video cameras was strategically installed all over Lhasa and other large cities in Tibet.

On October 1, 1987, *The New York Times*[16] reported: "In a rare Chinese acknowledgement of public dissent in Tibet, the Chinese press agency has reported a march by a group of Buddhist lamas calling for Tibet's independence. The agency said the march took place on Sunday in Lhasa, the capital of Tibet, which was occupied by the Chinese army in 1959. The New China News Agency said that 21 lamas and five other unidentified people paraded near the Jokhang Temple in Lhasa, the most sacred shrine of Tibetan Buddhism, shouting 'Tibet wants independence' and waving a traditional flag depicting the snow mountains and lions of Tibet."

The US newspaper added: "There were conflicting reports both in Lhasa and in Beijing today that several foreigners had been detained for questioning. The Foreign Affairs Office in Lhasa, the bureau designated to handle inquiries from foreign news agencies, said foreigners had taken part in the demonstration, but Laba Ciren [Lhakpa Tsering] said he was not aware of that. The demonstration came as Tibet Buddhism's highest religious figure, the Dalai Lama, was touring the United States, a visit that has prompted repeated protests by China."[17]

Xinhua reported that the Chinese embassy in Washington had expressed "deep regret and indignation," and that "[the US Congress] should not interfere in China's internal affairs and allow the Dalai Lama to conduct political activities aimed at advocating independence for Tibet and sabotaging the unity of China." Beijing denied allegations that some political prisoners were detained in Tibet stating that the notion of political prisoners did not exist in China. According to the Chinese government 974 people were detained in one jail and two re-education camps in Tibet (this included 964 common law prisoners and a handful of "anti-revolutionary criminals"). Xinhua also asserted that "according to Lhasa residents of Tibetan nationality … the Dalai Lama does not represent the Tibetan people."

Beijing took the protests extremely seriously. For the first (and last) time, a communist senior official wrote to a Tibetan leader in exile. On October 17, 1987, Yang Minfu, the Head of The United Front Work Department wrote to Gyalo Thondup, the Dalai Lama's brother. Referring to Thondup's visit to Beijing,[18] Minfu wrote: "I have learned about the two rounds of discussions you had with our comrades in the Second Bureau. Today, I would like to further discuss certain issues with you."[19] He immediately broached the Dalai Lama's address to the US Congress: "On September 19 this year, the Dalai Lama visited the United States and openly raised an outcry about 'Tibet's independence' on September 21 by propounding a 'Five Point Peace Plan' at the Congressional Human Rights Caucus. A few splittists in Lhasa supported the Dalai Lama's splittist activities and created disturbances on September 27 and October 1." This term "splittist" has constantly been used through the following years to characterise the Tibetan leader's activities, even after he has reiterated that he does not seek independence from China.

After the first demonstrations around the Bakhor, Beijing reacted: "The Central Government views with extreme seriousness the Dalai Lama's splittist activities and Lhasa disturbances." After reiterating China's "steadfast position," Yang Minfu quoted from an editorial of *The People's Daily*: "The Lhasa disturbances, fomented by a few splittists, are serious political incidents instigated and planned by the Dalai group. Their aim is to undermine the unity of the Motherland and sabotage the unity and stability in Tibet by supporting the Dalai's illegal splittist activities in foreign countries."

An important aspect of the 1987-1989 protest is that at the beginning at least, thousands of foreign visitors and media persons were present in the Tibetan capital and images of the repression which followed were reported the world over. Incidents continued to sporadically occur, which are said to have resulted in the loss of several Tibetan lives. Beginning 1988, the Chinese leadership became more and more nervous as they felt they were losing face in the world's eyes. The monks, the very same people they were supposed to have "liberated" from the clutches of the clergy, were now revolting against the "motherland." But worse for Beijing: if the situation was allowed to drift, China could follow the Soviet Union on the way to disintegration. The situation deteriorated in Tibet, finally ending by the massacre of hundreds of Tibetans on the Bakhor in Lhasa on March 6, 1989 and the proclamation of Martial Law on March 8, 1989.

The Case of Hu Jintao

However, before proceeding, it is necessary to look at the case of Hu Jintao, the future Chinese President. In 1988, the strong men in the Politburo were Li Peng and Qiao Shi, Hu Jintao's mentor. Qiao had visited Tibet in July. It is probably at that time that it was decided to appoint Hu Jintao to replace Wu Jinghua as Tibet's Party Chief. It was to be a crucial turn in Hu's career. He probably knew he had to show results in a very short time to repay the confidence placed in him by Qiao Shi. Hu knew he could not afford to fail. Had not Qiao Shi threatened of "merciless repression" if the demonstrations were not immediately stopped?

Hu Jintao took over the rebellious region on January 12, 1989. A Hong Kong paper *Kuang Chiao Ching* wrote at that time: "If he can stabilise the situation in Tibet that would, of course, be the first step towards a rapid rise in Hu Jintao's political fortunes. If he rules Tibet successfully, perhaps the question on everyone's mind in the near future could be: Will Hu Jintao become a superstar on China's political stage?"[20] On January 19, 1989, Hu had a meeting with the People's Liberation Army. During his speech, he spoke about the "the CCP Central Committee's new instructions on work in Tibet." Hu told the army: "We must strengthen control of monasteries and temples," a bad omen for the Tibetans.

A week later, a Beijing newspaper *Zhongguo Xinwen She* published an interview with Hu in which he described his two main tasks in Tibet: "To safeguard the unification of the motherland, adopt a clear-cut stand to oppose separatism, and stabilise the situation in Tibet," and then: "to continue to carry out economic construction, make redoubled efforts to develop the commodity economy." This would later be known as Hu's strategy of "grasping with both hands."

From that day, events moved very fast. On January 23, Hu visited the Tashilhunpo monastery in Shigatse. He was accompanied by the Panchen Lama, the second highest ranking Tibetan Lama after the Dalai Lama. The official occasion was the consecration of a *stupa* containing the mortal remains of one of the previous Panchen Lamas. To everyone's surprise, during the function, the Panchen Lama denounced the Communist Party's role in Tibet and said that "although there had been developments in Tibet since its liberation, this development had cost more dearly than its achievements. This mistake must never be repeated." Four days later, he passed away in mysterious circumstances. Though Tibetans believed he was murdered, it has never been proven. It is said the Panchen Lama had a serious quarrel with Qiao Shi just before he left for Tibet. Whether this was true or not, the stage was cleared for "merciless repression."

When a demonstration erupted on March 5, the People's Armed Police (PAP) quickly took control of the situation.

The Massacre at the Bakhor

In an article published in 1990 in *The Tibetan Review,*[21] the events which led to the imposition of martial law are recounted: "On March 5 [1989] three months before Tiananmen square, the People's Armed Police knew it had been given the right to kill. China's paramilitary force was marching into the centre of Tibet's capital, Lhasa, to begin a massacre that continued for days, leaving more than 450 monks, nuns and civilians dead. Thousands more were arrested and many tortured." It quotes Tang Daxian, an official reporter for some of media organisations, who had managed to escape to the West: "They knew the Tibetans were not armed as they were, and they knew they were free to kill them," he said. The Tibetan Review continues: "On the basis of secret official reports made available last week to *The Observer* by Tang, it now appears that the massacre in Tibet was provoked by members of the armed police dressed as Tibetans. The disguised police—whose purpose is to crush civil disorder—attacked and burned shops, offices, and stores, providing the authorities with the excuse that they were dealing with hooligans who threatened civil order."[22]

Martial law was finally declared in Lhasa on March 8, 1989. Three months later a similar scenario would occur in Beijing followed by the killings of thousands of students on the night of June 3 at the Tiananmen Square. The martial law in Lhasa was to last for 387 days. It was lifted on April 30, 1990. By that time, Hu Jintao, Tibet's Communist Party Secretary, had been promoted in Beijing; he was praised for his "immortal deeds" in maintaining order in China's largest minority area.

From Martial Law to the Tiananmen Events

The tragic events in Lhasa seem to have been a rehearsal for an even more important episode: the student rebellion on Tiananmen Square three months later. Hu Jintao told Xinhua news agency a few days after the events: "We should maintain vigilance against possible activity by the handful of separatists and strike them with relentless blows. We should mete out more severe punishment to those who would start troublemaking after the declaration of martial law."[23] His ruthless implementation of his bosses' orders and the subsequent replay of Lhasa events at Tiananmen Square proved he was a leader who could be relied upon. When, after the massacre at the Square, Jiang Zemin replaced Zhao Ziyang, he remembered this.

Hu was to stay on for four more years in Tibet, though the job was done in three months. Hu never liked Tibet. He once told a journalist he "disliked Tibet's altitude, climate and lack of culture." During the following months and years, he began shuttling between Lhasa and Beijing where the real power was. There was a common joke about Hu amongst Tibetan cadres: "Where is Hu?" The answer was: "Hu is in Beijing Hospital." He had to officially report sick each time he was going to Beijing!

During a visit to Tibet in 1990, Jiang Zemin echoed Hu's views: "It is necessary to strengthen education in patriotism and socialism in the light of conditions in China and Tibet, so as to make the students know from childhood that Tibet is an inalienable sacred part of the big family of the motherland, and that there will be no socialist new Tibet if there is no CCP." It appears that during Jiang Zemin's visit to Tibet, a close relationship was established between the general secretary and his future protégé. Did Hu save China which could have plunged into the "chaos" so feared by the Chinese emperors? Probably! Had Tibet been lost, no doubt other provinces such as Xinjiang would have followed in quick succession.

The Third Phase: March-April 2008

New protests started on March 10, 2008 when 500 monks of the Drepung monastery marched to Lhasa: they were commemorating the 49th anniversary of the 1959 uprising. Like in 1987-88, the clergy took the lead in the protests. This protest was followed the next day by the march of 14 monks of Sera Monastery towards the Jokhang Cathedral. As the repression mounted, more and more lay people and monks joined. Minor protests were also reported from Amdo region (today in Qinghai province).

The next day, 600 monks from Sera monastery marched peacefully to the Tibetan capital. They were also tear-gassed by police and many were arrested. The same method was used by the PAP in Sera: the water supply of the monastery was cut off and restaurants in the area closed. On March 12, when two monks from Drepung cut their wrists, other monks from Sera monastery began a demonstration. During the first three days, the main events occurred around Lhasa. Local authorities however considered the happenings as "a direct challenge to the long term stability of Tibet." During the next few days, contrary to the first two periods,[24] the unrest spread to the entire Tibetan plateau. This was the first time in the history of Tibet since 1950 that the three traditional provinces were aflame at the same time.

On March 13, when a few hundreds of monks from Ganden monastery, together with a few nuns, came to Lhasa to stage a peaceful protest, they were stopped by the police. Later that day, the three Great Monasteries of Drepung, Ganden and Sera were closed. The next day—March 14, 2008—will remain etched in the history of protests in Tibet. It was subsequently termed "the 3/14 incident" by Beijing, probably to make it sound like a terrorist attack against the People's Republic of China. In the morning, about one hundred monks from Ramoche monastery began to demonstrate against the arrest of the monks on the previous days. Once again they were stopped and beaten by the police. This infuriated the Tibetan passers-by. From then on, the situation went out of control.

Soon after, a large-scale demonstration involving tens of thousands of people lead to a confrontation between Tibetans and the PAP. It was reported that on March 14, the ban on firing weapons was lifted. Police and the PAP were free to shoot at will. Robert Barnett, a scholar from Columbia University, later wrote the details of the events for the *New York Review of Books*:[25] "Unlike the great monasteries, Ramoche is in the heart of Lhasa, and opens onto a busy market street in one of the few areas of the city that remains a largely Tibetan quarter. Members of the public, apparently aroused by rumours that monks detained that Monday had been beaten in custody, began to attack the police and a small squad of PAP sent in to support them." Barnett's narration continues: "The police and soldiers were pelted with stones, their cars were burned and, pursued by a group of stone-throwing youths, they fled. No reinforcements were sent into the area for at least three hours (one Western journalist who witnessed the events saw no police for twenty-four hours), though they were waiting on the outskirts."

The attack against the police was a strong symbol of the resentment against Chinese governance. Barnett writes: "The rapid increase of migrants in Tibetan towns (they already were 34 per cent of the Lhasa population when official figures were last made available in 2000, and this figure probably excludes temporary residents and the military) had created uneasy resentment—until then silent—among the indigenous population. About a thousand Chinese-owned shops were set on fire by rioters." Barnett quotes *The Economist's* correspondent: "almost every [Chinese] business was either burned, looted, destroyed, smashed into, the property therein hauled out into the streets, piled up, burned. It was an extraordinary outpouring of ethnic violence of a most unpleasant nature to watch." Fifty years of bitterness and anger against the "colonisation" of Tibet could finally express itself in the street.

Barnett continues: "Later, the PAP moved in, shooting from time to time, leading to an unknown number of casualties. The exile Tibetan government has said that eighty Tibetans were shot dead in Lhasa, while the Chinese government says that its forces never opened fire … By the official count, one thousand Tibetans were detained in Lhasa alone, and the punishment of those deemed guilty of offences is expected to be ferocious—to be handled according to the principles of 'quick approval, quick arrest, quick trial, quick execution' according to Zhang Qingli, the current Party secretary of the Tibet Autonomous Region."

The unrest occurred as many local Party cadres were attending the annual National People's Congress in Beijing. From Beijing, the Tibetan Autonomous authorities immediately blamed the Dalai Lama. Even Premier Wen Jiabao accused the Tibetan Leader to have masterminded the violence for sabotaging the forthcoming Olympic Games. This was denied by the Dalai Lama. Interestingly, while details of the riots of 1959 and 1989 were known only months later, this time, thanks to mobile phones and other video cameras (even if calls to India were monitored by the Public Security

Bureau), hundreds of photos and many videos reached India and the West. They were later circulated on the Internet.

The Reaction of the Dalai Lama

A few weeks later the Tibetan leader addressed an open letter to his "Chinese brothers and sisters." He wrote:

> In the light of the recent developments in Tibet, I would like to share with you my thoughts concerning relations between the Tibetan and Chinese peoples, and make a personal appeal to all of you. I am deeply saddened by the loss of life in the recent tragic events in Tibet. I am aware that some Chinese have also died. I feel for the victims and their families and pray for them. The recent unrest has clearly demonstrated the gravity of the situation in Tibet and the urgent need to seek a peaceful and mutually beneficial solution through dialogue. Even at this juncture I have expressed my willingness to the Chinese authorities to work together to bring about peace and stability.[26]

But it was probably too late, for the Communist leaders were shocked beyond words by the events in Lhasa and then all over the plateau. Who in China believed the words of the Dalai Lama when he said:

> Chinese brothers and sisters, I assure you I have no desire to seek Tibet's separation. Nor do I have any wish to drive a wedge between the Tibetan and Chinese peoples. On the contrary, my commitment has always been to find a genuine solution to the problem of Tibet that ensures the long-term interests of both Chinese and Tibetans. My primary concern, as I have repeated time and again, is to ensure the survival of the Tibetan people's distinctive culture, language and identity. As a simple monk who strives to live his daily life according to Buddhist precepts, I assure you of the sincerity of my personal motivation.[27]

A few days later in another statement, he asked for an independent enquiry into the events: "I would also request you [Governments and NGOs] to encourage the sending of an independent international body, to investigate the unrest and its underlying causes, as well as allowing the media and international medical teams to visit the affected areas. Their presence will not only instil a sense of reassurance in the Tibetan people, but will also exercise a restraining influence on the Chinese authorities." However, there was no response from Beijing.

Unlike at the end of the 1980s, when the protests were limited to Central Tibet, this time the unrest spread to all Tibetan inhabited areas, more particularly in the Eastern and North-eastern provinces of Kham and Amdo. According to Tibetan sources, some 200 Tibetans lost their lives and thousands were arrested. Several Chinese were reported to have been killed on March 14.

This was certainly a major turning point especially as far as the negotiations between Dharamsala and Beijing were concerned. Months later, voices of dissidence were heard in China, but they remained negligible. One such voice is Zhang Boshu, who, soon after the riots of March-April 2008, wrote an essay on *The Way to Resolve the Tibet Issue*.

Zhang Boshu, after obtaining a PhD degree in philosophy in 1991, started teaching at the Philosophy Institute of the Chinese Academy of Social Sciences. His biography says: "In recent years he has striven to understand the lessons of success and failure in the history of the past century of China's democratic transition and institutional modernisation. He has gradually settled upon criticism of twentieth century Chinese despotism as his main research topic."[28] Zhang's first question is "How did the Tibet issue arise?" He believes that this problem plaguing the Party for the past 50 years was created "by the Chinese Communist Party itself as the ruler of China." Such dissent is a new development though it has remained limited in China.

Conclusions: Resentment Remains and Self-immolations

The latest phase of show of resentment has been marked by more than 140 self-immolations since 2010; it occurred mainly in Eastern Tibet (former provinces of Kham and Amdo), with a large percentage of monks "offering" their lives for the Tibetan cause. In conclusion, though China had announced that it had "liberated" Tibet in 1950-51, it is clear that a lot of resentment is still present today in the former provinces of Tibet (U-Tsang, Kham and Amdo). Today, Beijing has found a more radical solution to solve the issue: 15 million Chinese Hans have come to Tibet in 2014. It has become the largest amusement park in the world, what we call a Disneyland of Snows. Beijing promotes Tibet thus: "Tibet with its mystery is the spiritual Garden of Eden and is longed by travellers home and abroad. Only by stepping on the snowy plateau, can one be baptised by its splendour, culture, folklore, life, snow mountains, saint mountains, sacred lakes, residences with local characteristics and charming landscape."[29] Some see it more as a large reservation on the model of the Native Americans! Will the problem be solved thus or will it explode again? It is difficult to predict, though it is clear that the resentment is still latent.

Notes

1. For the text of the 17-Point Agreement, see http://www.claudearpi.net/maintenance/uploaded_pics/1951AgreementonMeasuresforthePeacefulLiberationofTibet.pdf
2. George N. Patterson, *Requiem for Tibet* (London: Aurum Press, 1990), p. 154.
3. Patterson, *Requiem for Tibet.*
4. *The Dalai Lama's Press Statements*, Statement issued at Tezpur, April 18, 1959, see http://www.claudearpi.net/maintenance/uploaded_pics/Tezpur.pdf
5. Gyaltse Namgyal Wandue, *Political and Military History of Tibet* (New Delhi: Paljor Publications, 2013).
6. Wandue, *Political and Military History of Tibet.*
7. History Leading up to March 10, 1959, see http://www.tibet.org/Why/march10.html
8. Communiqué on the Revolt, New China News Agency, Peking, March 28, 1959, see www.claudearpi.net/maintenance/.../Communique_on_the_Revolt.pdf
9. Ling Nai-Min, *Tibetan Sourcebook* (Hong Kong: Union Research Institute, 1964), p. 348.
10. Major S. L. Chhibber from the Indian Frontier Administrative Service.
11. Prime Minister's Statement in the Lok Sabha On March 23, 1959. See http://www.claudearpi.net/maintenance/uploaded_pics/1959LS_Statement_March.pdf
12. Prime Minister's Statement in the Lok Sabha.
13. Ling Nai-Min, *Tibetan Sourcebook*, p. 349.
14. Five Point Peace Plan (Address to the US Congressional Human Rights Caucus), .see http://www.dalailama.com/messages/tibet/five-point-peace-plan
15. The future President of China.
16. "Protest by Lamas to Free Tibet," *The New York Times*, October 1, 1989.
17. "Protest by Lamas to Free Tibet."
18. Gyalo Thondup was in China during the September 1987 riots in Lhasa.
19. For the full text of the Yang Minfu Memorandum, see http://www.claudearpi.net/index.php?nav=documents&id=3&lang=1
20. See http://www.rediff.com/news/2002/dec/10spec1.htm
21. "450 Tibetans murdered in Lhasa riot of March '89—Chinese journalist presents documentary evidence," *The Tibetan Review*, September 1990.
22. *The Tibetan Review.*
23. http://www.rediff.com/news/2002/dec/10spec1.htm
24. March 1959 and 1987-1989.
25. Robert Barnett, "Thunder from Tibet," in *New York Review of Books*, vol. 55, no. 9, May 29, 2008. See http://www.nybooks.com/articles/21391
26. "An Appeal to the Chinese People," see: http://www.dalailama.com/messages/tibet/appeal-to-the-chinese-people
27. "An Appeal to the Chinese People."
28. Zhang Boshu, "The way to resolve the Tibet issue," see http://www.tibet-china-conference.org/content/pdf_chn/Zhang_Boshu_english.pdf
29. *China Tibet Online,* http://eng.tibet.cn/2010hb/xw/201308/t20130801_1914973.html

2. The Protest Movement and Political Change in Tajikistan

Kamoluddin Abdullaev

Tajikistan has experienced one of the most difficult state-building projects among the former Soviet Republics. Since the late Soviet period the country has experienced a rapid rise in political activism, civil war and ethnic cleansings, an internationally led peace process, the integration of opposition forces into government, disarmament of former combatants, moderation of radical Islamism and their inclusion, redistribution of power amongst regions, promotion of multi-partyism and freedoms and recent exclusion and dramatic slide to destabilisation and the return of authoritarianism and repression.

Almost immediately after the collapse of the USSR, Tajikistan became a scene of brutal civil war, taking place in one of the global hubs of religiously motivated political struggle, militancy, mass cross-border refugee flows, insurgency, and drug trafficking. In 2000, Tajikistan with the help of the international community broke out of its cycle of violence and economic decline after ending the civil war through a negotiated settlement. The country was making modest progress toward stability. However, the heavy burden of socio-economic problems, in addition to the conflict in neighbouring Afghanistan-Pakistan, series of protests and "colour revolution" across Eurasia and "jihadi" challenge presented even bigger problems for Tajikistan.

This paper focuses on social movements in Tajikistan, beginning with the late Soviet period to the present. It discusses the social impulse for protest, considers the strategies of social movements, looks at the institutional response to protest, and finally puts forward a question: what is the impact of the structure and development of the state on social movements itself?

Why Tajikistan?

Tajikistan is the poorest and only Persian-speaking country among the post-Soviet independent states. The Tajik autonomous republic that was formed within Uzbekistan in 1924 and given a status of the full-fledged Soviet republic in 1929, became completely independent in 1991. This country occupies the south-eastern part of the region which was called Central Asia by the nineteenth-century Russians and Europeans. Today Central Asia is a region of both a growing strategic significance and challenge. This region is strategic due to its proximity to the war against the Taliban and Al Qaeda and close affiliation with the major Eurasian actors like Russia, China, Iran, Pakistan, and India. Tajikistan's place is unique in this region. It shares Afghanistan's longest northern border and is divided from Pakistan by a narrow (15-60 km wide) strip of Afghan land. This makes it the closest post-Soviet territory to the Afghan-Pak conflict zone. Furthermore, Tajiks share ethnic ties with Afghanistan's largest minority, as some 27 per cent of the Afghan population is Tajik. Their number is even more than the number of Tajiks in Tajikistan.

Physical factors make Tajikistan vulnerable to conflict for it is surrounded by more powerful countries, and its territory is divided by mountains, into separate regions with specific political features, and peripheral areas that historically had closer links with neighbouring countries than with the capital. Tajikistan's position between South Asia and the hydrocarbon-rich Caspian basin as well as Tajiks' ethno-cultural ties to Iranians, Russians, Afghans, Pakistanis and Chinese make this country a strategic region.

"Tajik Civil War": Who Are the Actors?

During the late Soviet period, Tajikistan, like other republics of the USSR, experienced unparalleled nationalist mobilisation. The communist leadership could do nothing but let cultural revivalism and religious rebirth grow in Tajikistan. In 1989, the Tajik language was recognised as official and even a return to the classic alphabet (which is what Tajiks call the Arabic alphabet) was proclaimed. The first democratic secular organisation in Tajikistan was formed in September 1989 under the name *Rastokhez*. *Rastokhez* called for greater autonomy for Tajikistan, Tajik cultural revival and pan-Persian solidarity with the Tajiks of Afghanistan and Uzbekistan as well as the Persians of Iran. The reputation of this nationalist movement was seriously damaged in February 1990, when public rallies protesting the relocation to and housing in Tajikistan of Armenian refugees left homeless by the war in Nagorno-Karabakh in January 1990 turned into anarchy and violence. The events of February 1990, which also constituted the first public rally of Tajiks since the revolution of 1917, left a bitter taste for the public and resulted in mass outmigration of Russians. These events were the first sign of the approaching chaos and collapse of Soviet rule in Tajikistan. Though the involvement of *Rastokhez* in instigating the hostility was doubtful, the organisation nevertheless was blamed for stimulating public unrest and violence directed against the local Russian population, which changed its public perception.

The competition for power began soon after Tajikistan declared its independence in September 1991. The first popular elections were held in November 1991 when Rakhmon Nabiev (Communist Party leader in 1982-1986) won a majority. The opposition—made up of a coalition including the Democratic Party and Islamic Renaissance Party (IRP)—contested the results and organised public demonstrations in Dushanbe. In March 1992, the demonstrations continued, and a counterforce composed mainly of governmental supporters from Kulob and Leninabad regions began to assemble. Open armed clashes between the two blocks erupted in early May, when the opposition captured key governmental installations in the capital. To reduce tensions, a compromise agreement was made allowing Nabiev to remain President, but providing opposition representatives a place in the so-called Government of National Reconciliation. This solution was short-lived. Nabiev resigned on September 7 to be replaced by Iskandarov Akbarsho. On October 23-24, 1992 heavy battles between pro-Nabiev and pro-opposition forces shook the capital causing hundreds of civilian deaths. On November 10 Iskandarov called a special session (known as the 16th) of the Supreme Soviet in Khujand which on November 18 accepted his resignation and elected a Kulabi, Emomali Rakhmonov (known as Emomali Rahmon since March 2007), as Supreme Soviet Chairman. After opposition forces were routed from Dushanbe, on December 14, 1992 Rakhmonov took his post in the capital.

From spring 1992 onwards, the conflict spread from Dushanbe to the periphery, and its "ruralisation" took place. State institutes began collapsing while political activists lost control of the situation to the benefit of semi-criminal "people's generals." Arms from Afghanistan and arsenals of the former Soviet Army turned the Tajik conflict into bloody chaos. From 1992 to 1997, violence ravaged through Khatlon, the Karategin Valley, and areas surrounding Dushanbe. Gradually, the war took on an interregional character, pitting the Popular Front ("Sitodi Melli")—led by

Kulobi field commanders, backed by Khujandis, Hisoris and Uzbeks from Khatlon—against groups originating mainly from the Karategin Valley and Mountainous Badakshan (sometimes referred to as "Gharmis")—united in the Rescuing the Motherland group ("Najoti Vatan"), later the United Tajik Opposition (UTO).

The Tajik civil war showed a tendency toward internationalisation. Islamic delegates from neighbouring Uzbekistan, Afghanistan, North Caucasus, and even Iran were present at mass demonstrations in Dushanbe. Some of them later formed the backbone of the "jihad" waged against the pro-Communist government. Russian officers and Uzbekistan's political elites provided military support to the governmental side.

However major actors were local. The Tajik war was neither primordial war of regions, nor a political parties-led violent ideological dispute, not to mention "war of secularists on Islamic fundamentalists." It was not a big powers' violent clash on the Tajik soil either. It was a war of regional—second echelon—post-Communist political entrepreneurs who used potency of apolitical and pejorative "field commanders" (warlords), ethno-territorial, and quasi-religious (Sufi) networks in order to secure, in various degrees, mass support in respective (mostly southern) areas. Southern Tajikistan, in particular Vakhsh Valley, has been a place where various Tajik and Uzbek groups were involuntarily settled during the period from the mid-1920s to the 1950s to cultivate much needed cotton there. The major conflict erupted between these communities.

As a result of the brutal civil war, up to 50,000 people lost their lives and more than 650,000 people—one-tenth of the population—were displaced. More than 35,000 homes were destroyed. The total war damage is estimated to be $7 billion.

Peacemaking: A Success or a Failure?

Unaware of the realities in Tajikistan, the West provided passive support to the opposition, viewing its resistance as a justified political protest of the devoted Muslims against the Communist rule. As the violence continued, the international community intervened and stopped the conflict.

An internationally facilitated peace process under the aegis of the UN and with the participation of Russia and Iran began in April 1994. Representatives of Afghanistan, Iran, Kazakhstan, Kyrgyzstan, Pakistan, Russia, Uzbekistan, Turkmenistan, the OSCE and the OIC served as observers in the Inter-

Tajik negotiations. The series of talks between the government of President Rakhmonov and the United Tajik Opposition ended on June 27, 1997 with the signing in Moscow of the *General Agreement on the Establishment of Peace and National Accord*. The UN opted for a relatively narrow but realistic peacemaking formula that focused on ending warfare. Because of this "security first" approach, the interests of some political forces (regions, parties, national communities) were not represented in the negotiations. The UTO and the Government both defended minimalist positions to reach compromise. The issues and problems that caused demonstrations five years earlier (e.g., political rights and freedoms, equality of sub-ethnic groups, etc.) were not addressed properly.

The assessments of the Tajik peace vary. The UN considers the Tajik peace settlement as one of the most successful they have ever sponsored. Dushanbe and many Tajiks would agree with this judgement, as they believe the peace process saved the nation from a catastrophe and helped national consolidation. Yet many in the West and Tajikistan itself consider the Tajik peace an exclusive bargaining deal between the two regional forces represented by pro-Communist Kulabis and Gharmi-dominated Islamists, who enriched themselves and attained positions of power in the wake of the peace process.

While a host of sources of conflict exist in post-war Tajikistan, the society demonstrates a low structural vulnerability to violence or a resumption of war. This is largely due to the existence of a consensus among elite groups and political entrepreneurs concerning the necessity of protecting the national state-building project and because of the successful distribution of "war-spoils"—positions and resources—between them. However this consensus is not based on an equitable distribution of wealth and resources among all Tajik regions and stratum of society. The Tajik state and society continue to have little potential to manage or contain conflict. There are few Tajik institutions that can play a mediating role—opposition political parties, independent media, an effective judiciary, an active civil society all lack capacity. At the regional level the threat of conflict is also significant due to the absence of adequate mediating mechanisms between Tajikistan and its neighbours. The 1997 peace agreement envisioned reconciliation in Tajikistan a short and mid-term only.

State Response: Calming Islamism

The most valuable and instructive part of the Tajik experience relates to the search for the most effective formula for dealing with religion-based political activism. Rapid rise of Islamic protest activism throughout the 1990s forced local elites to respond differently. Uzbekistan adopted a law "On liberty of conscience and religious organisations" on May 1, 1998, while Tajikistan a year later amended its Constitution's article 28. Both measures were of the opposite content. Uzbekistan confirmed previous restrictions and added the right of state to limit liberty of conscience "if it is needed for securing national safety, civil order, life, health, ethics, rights and liberties of other citizens." This law has legalised a severe oppression of the Islamic activism in Uzbekistan and laid the foundation for further marginalisation and radicalisation of IMU.

Meanwhile, in 1999, Tajikistan amended its Constitution, authorising the formation of, "among others, parties of a democratic, religious, or atheistic character." This legal framework is poorly formulated, because it suggests that parties can be either democratic or religious, but not both. This formal imperfection underscores the hasty manner in which the Tajik Constitution was reformed in the aftermath of the civil war. The changes to the Constitution were made under the pressure of international guarantors of the Tajik peace process and the activity of the Islamic Renaissance Party was legalised. Today, Tajikistan is the only state in the region where the Islamic movement, after ten years of open confrontation, opted to participate in the political process, within quasi-democratic structures. The Islamic party was legalised, while secularism remained central to Tajikistan's Constitution.

The departure of IRPT from its original objective of an "Islamic state" to "Islamic society"[1] may, hypothetically, contribute to the growing polarisation and split within the Tajik Islamist camp and gradual radicalisation of the fundamentalist wing, dissatisfied with the "corrupt" leadership. Thus far, the leadership of IRPT managed to keep the party within the framework of secular legislature. Furthermore, the legalisation provided political space for believers in Tajikistan, thus creating an opportunity for dialogue and dampening the threat of terrorism. However, legalisation of IRPT has not contributed to the overall liberalisation of the political life in the region. The IRPT as well as secular Central Asian parties emerged from the Soviet past, with no tradition of democratic development and political dialogue. The party of the Tajik Islamists is built on both the model of Muslim Brotherhood and Communist party. It is based on loyalty to the leader and rife with corruption and cronyism.

Even though the important dilemma of secularism versus Islamism remains unresolved in Tajik politics in the long term, Tajikistan represents an example of a relative success, in which the conventional Sunni Islamist movement was able to secure a stable electorate within their own country. Even under the influence of the Soviet-Afghan war, Iranian revolution, and Soviet atheism, Tajik Islamists never joined transnational terrorist network, but focused on national politics with the goal of replacing corrupt post-communist ruling elites, while resisting localism and ethnic nationalism. The inclusion of IRPT represents an example of a successful bargaining of the government and Islamic militants. It showed that "Islamic politics" is not inevitably and hopelessly radical, anti-systemic, and violent.

State Response to the Post-war Internal Disturbances

Central Asia and Tajikistan in particular experienced relative calm beginning late 2001 and many attributed it to the coalition success in defeating the Taliban. This calm did not last long, however, with violence breaking out in the spring of 2009. In May 2009, one of the former opposition field commanders Mullo Abdullo (Rahimov) came back to Tavildara region of Tajikistan. Having refused the peace agreement that ended the Tajik civil war in 1997, Mullo Abdullo had fled to Afghanistan with his fighters. After the US launched the operation "Enduring Freedom" in 2001, Mullo Abdullo, along with some Taliban fighters, fled to Pakistan's tribal areas. His reappearance in Tajikistan in May 2009 caused panic, with the local media portraying him as the Tajik Osama bin Laden. Upon his return home, Mullo Abdullo tried to establish contact with the government and former opposition leaders. However, neither the government nor former UTO leaders were interested in a dialogue with him.

The next wave of instability in Tajikistan broke out in August 2010, when a group of 25 prisoners escaped from the State National Security Committee's detention centre in Dushanbe, just blocks away from the presidential residence. The escapees had been charged with plotting against the state and sentenced to a long-term imprisonment. This outbreak of violence in Tajikistan seemed to confirm the alarmist prognosis that the conflict in Afghanistan was spilling over to Central Asia and that Central Asia was fast becoming the next hotbed for jihadi activities. The Tajik government, for once, did not spare the opportunity to portray the events as the Tajik government's successful fight against terrorism. Virtually all Central Asian regimes supported this alarmist assessment.

In fact, people in Central Asia are increasingly associating their future with growing Taliban and even Al Qaeda influence. Even if the threat is not real, people's overall perception is pessimistic. The threat of radical Islamism emanating from Afghanistan-Pakistan has been deeply entrenched in the political culture of Afghan neighbours since the Soviet-Afghan war. It justified the building of foreign bases and enhancing military cooperation within the framework of the region's major international organisations led by Russia and China: Collective Security Treaty Organisation (CSTO) and Shanghai Cooperation Organisation (SCO), respectively. Accordingly, outsiders see Central Asia through the same lens of radical Islam and as an arena for potentially "another Afghanistan." Alteration of this paradigm is a tough challenge and major domestic and international stakeholders, including Russia and China, seem unwilling to dispense this seemingly overstated threat, which has served them as a universal political tool in achieving their goals.

In the Central Asian context, factors that have driven the conflict in the past may paradoxically play a positive role in conflict prevention and reconciliation. For example, *mahalgaroi* (localism) and clanism that divide Tajiks was partly responsible for the Tajik civil war in 1992-1997. As a result, Tajiks strive, albeit unsuccessfully, to get rid of localism and build a civic identity and pluralism in politics. However, these ethno-territorial communities (mahals) as "organic" and stable kin-based associations have served as a useful conflict prevention mechanism. It was these ethno-territorial ties that laid the basis for a negotiated settlement between the major peace-spoilers and armed groups, namely Kulabis and Gharmis, during the civil war. This deal excluded other groups from the power-sharing arrangement, which many experts view as the major shortfall of the Tajik Peace Agreement. Despite its shortfalls, however, the peace agreement has ensured peace and stability in Tajikistan since 1997.

Similarly, the recent penetration of militants from Afghanistan and Pakistan into Tajikistan did not evolve into a full-blown crisis because of the bargaining between the two civil wartime factions, namely President Rahmon's supporters and Gharmi commanders Shoh Iskandarov and Mirzokhuja Ahmadov. This bargaining neutralised the threat of importing jihad to Tajikistan at a relatively low cost and without a third-party intervention.

In July 2012 protest movement erupted in Mountainous Badakhshan Autonomous Region of eastern Tajikistan. The Tajik authorities dispatched hundreds of troops, along with helicopter gunships and armoured vehicles, to the provincial capital Khorog city to detain Tolib Ayombekov, a deputy commander of a Tajik-Afghan border unit and an opposition leader during the 1992-1997 Tajikistan civil war, and several of his associates. They were suspected of killing Maj. Gen. Abdullo Nazarov, local head of the State Committee for National Security. The agency had long accused Ayombekov's associates of smuggling drugs, tobacco, and precious stones. Forty people had been killed and dozens injured in this special operation in Khorog. During this military action Tajik authorities have periodically blocked Internet, mobile, and landline connections to Badakhshan province. The head of the state communications service, Beg Zukhurov (Beg Saburi), claimed that a stray bullet had severed telephone, mobile, and Internet connections to the region. He rejected the information of some media on communications blocked by Tajik national security agencies.

Both in Gharm in 2009-2011 and in Khorog in 2012 the security situation had been resolved through the use of familiar the civil wartime bargaining of field commanders, combined with state-led violence against peace-spoilers. The Kulabis occupy top positions in the Tajik government, including the power ministries. This has contributed to the endemic corruption in Tajikistan. However, the Kulabi commanders were among those who relentlessly chased Mullo Abdullo and his men in Gharm until they were eliminated in April 2011. Jihadis were defeated not by a professional army equipped with hi-tech weaponry, but by communalists armed with light weapons. Authoritarian rule has been instrumental in defeating Islamic militants and Al Qaeda emissaries in the region. Similarly in Khorog, the Kulabi dominated government calmed the situation in July 2012 and made a deal with local pro-separatist leaders, albeit killing dozens of innocents, but preventing a mass protest movement on the very Afghan border.

Thus authoritarianism is both a problem and solution while dealing with conflict and conflict resolution in Central Asia. Under what conditions does a given factor serve as a conflict trigger and under what conditions as conflict preventer is a tough challenge that conflict analysis faces in the Central Asian context.

State Response to a Potential "Colour Revolution"

Not surprisingly, the Tajik and Uzbek governments' answer to the conflict in Afghanistan-Pakistan and occurrences of protest movements worldwide has been growing authoritarianism and serious violations of human rights and freedoms. In order to prevent technologically induced political mobilisation, in recent years the governmental authorities of Tajikistan not only block domestic access to popular social networking but also monitor the Internet access of individuals. The websites could have been blocked after a plea to join the anti-government demonstration on October 10, 2014 was published on Facebook. These anonymous calls and rude comments posted online about President Rahmon and his family, led to the closure of more than 200 websites, including Facebook, VKontakte, YouTube, several Russian-language news websites and the Russian version of Wikipedia. The head of the governmental Communications Service, Beg Saburi, denied his ministry's involvement in the blockings but noted that some websites "are overly politicised and instead of promoting peace and harmony in our society incite conflicts and post extremist calls and remarks." Referring to peace and harmony and President Rahmon's personal contribution in bringing stability in Tajikistan

There was no response to the call for a rally on October 10 that was attributed to the opposition journalist Dodojon Atovulloev, who currently resides in Germany, and the former businessman Umarali Kuvvatov, who also lived outside Tajikistan. These individuals, who are practically unknown to Tajikistanis, claim to have set up a Group 24 which, they say, includes many prominent Tajik politicians. Nevertheless, since its appearance, the Group has failed to move beyond posting calls on the Internet. Umarali Kuvvatov was shot and killed on March 5, 2015 in Istanbul.

Later some banned websites were reopened as blocking certain websites has proved to be a pointless government tactic: Tajik Internet users, having learnt from their previous website-blocking experience, actively share bypassing techniques on the Internet by posting links to proxy servers and gateway software downloads.[2]

Conclusion

The bloody Tajik civil war exemplifies the failure of politics by ordinary means. The experience of this war makes Tajikistan less prone to mass protest movement. And this is not surprising as 50,000 persons lost their lives and more than 650,000 people—one-tenth of the population—were displaced. Swayed by a host of factors, including the powerful argument that a continuation of conflict would lead to an irreversible disintegration of the Tajik state, which was contrary to both sides' nationalist aspirations, the warring factions signed the General Agreement on the Establishment of Peace and National Accord in 1997.

The major response to that war was disbelief and a taboo to any kind of public political protest and anathema to opposition widely accepted by society. Consequently, the consolidation of central authority was seen by international community and most of Tajiks as bringing peace in the country. The post-war recovery has not been accompanied by an adequate increase in pluralism and public participation in the political decision-making process. Procuring immediate stability as a goal was very successful in stopping the war, but it has not yet been as successful in establishing a more democratic system of governance and long-lasting peace and stability.

The most valuable and instructive part of the Tajik experience relates to the search for the most effective formula for dealing with religion-based political activism. The Tajik model of inclusion seems preferable and a more promising form of dealing with Muslim policies in Central Asia compared to the "combat/control" model proposed by Tashkent. The severe repression of opposition, instead of weakening the Islamist militancy, has strengthened and radicalised the Islamist groups in Uzbekistan. So far, the inclusion of Islamic policies has not led to clericalisation and a clash with secularism in Tajikistan. Dialogue and inclusion are unlikely to help Islamists come to power in Tajikistan or in any other Central Asian states. Instead, inclusion depends mostly on the efficiency of secular regimes and their ability to intercept the initiative from Islamists in an open and democratic environment. To avoid a slide back to militancy, there is a need, in addition to supporting national economic development, of providing advocacy to all political movements committed to acting legally.

The main threat to Central Asian security is not radicalisation of Muslim policies but the general failure of political and economic transformation, as well as the rise in authoritarianism and widespread corruption. Lack of cooperation between Central Asian governments and rapid militarisation of the region further deteriorates the situation. Local regimes and their close non-Muslim neighbours—China and Russia—identify radical Islamist mobilisation as a threat to national security interests. A consequence of this is a rapid, burdensome and dangerous militarisation of the region.

Governments have chosen repression as the only response to any kind of dissent. This concentration of fear, violence, mistrust, and mismanagement is the most alarming problem of the region.

Tajikistan is not a place that is witness to protests these days. The Tajik government and part of the society are right to worry about the possibility of a mass protest movement that may trigger the resumption of a civil war in Tajikistan. "Revolutionary" removal of Central Asian ruling regimes will unleash the forces, including religious groups, political movements, ethnic communities, and former combatants that these regimes hold under control. These disenfranchised groups may utilise the slogans of democracy to further their interests, thus destabilising the whole region. It is also right to assume that many Tajiks today want change and feel inspired by events in Arab countries, Ukraine and Kyrgyzstan. They believe that authoritarian rulers can be removed and stability should not be viewed as the only objective for the international community while regulating the conflicts in the region under study.

In today's Tajikistan the state and society demonstrate a surprisingly low structural vulnerability to a resumption of war. Yet the country faces external and internal threats of different intensity, and possesses few effective tools to deal with them. The lack of effective regional conflict mediation mechanisms or Tajik institutions that can play a mediating role should internal conflicts arise, makes Tajikistan vulnerable to a rapid escalation of internal or external tensions. The challenge is to promote both a strong government and political pluralism. Genuine reforms are key to keeping Tajikistan stable.

There is, unfortunately, no easy fix or universal formula in solving the age-long dilemma of ensuring security and promoting development. Eventually, political change is dependent on how good protesters are in framing and managing protests, and how the state and international community at large are going to respond.

Notes

1 Farangis Najibullah, *Tajikistan's Islamic Renaissance Party Rebrands, Using Social Projects To Reach Voters,* http://www.rferl.org/content/tajikistan_irp_islamic_renaissance_party/16799265.html

2. Source: *Russia Beyond the Headlines*, http://rbth.com/news/2014/10/06/tajik_authorities_block_200_websites_for_calling_for_anti-government_ral_40370.html)

3. Water Resource Management in Central Asia: An Issue of Social Conflict

Aidar Amrebayev and Aigul Akhanova

Although experts assert that unequal distribution of water resources and water shortage have an influence on the potential for social conflict in Central Asia, recent sources demonstrated that water wastage, excessive water demand, ineffective treaties and water management also have an influence on the economic condition of local people. Thus economic issues have the potential to influence social conflicts in Central Asia. Are the five states of Central Asia (Kazakhstan, Uzbekistan, Turkmenistan, Tajikistan and Kyrgyzstan) capable of solving regional water and economic issues for their common interest? What is the best model of water management for Central Asian states to reduce the potential for social conflicts? These are some of the questions addressed by the paper.

Potential for Conflict in Central Asia

Nowadays, social processes develop quite dynamically. The ongoing transformation of the world order, ideological interaction, interpenetration of various social, political and economic models influences the dynamics of global processes. All these factors also influence the level of social conflict potential in each region. The term "conflict" has several definitions. According to A. Kibanov, "Conflict is a social phenomenon, the way people communicate in case of their incompatible views, positions and interests, confrontation of two or more interrelated sides which have their own aims."[1] Whereas, according to E. Utkin, "Conflict is a clash of opposing positions, opinions and ideas that people try to regulate by using persuasion or actions in emotional state."[2] Thus "social conflict is an open confrontation, clash of two or more actors and participants of social interaction, where incompatible needs, interests and values are the main reasons."[3]

Today, the outcomes of the global confrontation of the new world order, taking into consideration the clashing interests of the global players, such as Russia, the West, China and the Muslim world, have an influence on Central Asian countries. Central Asia becomes an object of a new "great game." There are some external forces which can use destabilisation in the region for their own interests and initiate protests. "Models of protests" can be different, for instance, "colour revolutions," "protection of the Russian world," border conflicts, property protection, corruption, inefficiency of public authorities, information warfare and destructive network influence on governments. There are various external forces that use media as an instrument to organise protests against existing political regimes. They can use "Twitter revolutions" at any time even in developed states.

In addition to this, Central Asian states realise various economic, political and social models with a different result. There is a huge imbalance in the development of various countries and their models. There are various regimes in the region where weak and unstable states can be a source of instability. Kyrgyz "colour revolutions" and events in Osh in 1990 can be cited as examples. Moreover, states face the challenge of power transition and try to find the best model of development. For example, Uzbekistan's possible orientation to the West can face a negative reaction from Russia and China. Also, society does not participate in policy decision-making and external forces try to influence them using propaganda. Intermittent national traditions of political and legal culture create a situation when people are absolutely indifferent towards political and socio-economic processes in their country. External forces use public consciousness and spread political myths and radical ideologies. Historically, water resources have been influencing stability in the region, especially in the region with uneven distribution of water resources. Thus water and energy issues are always at the centre of attention and a cause of conflict between states. It is worth noting that there is no ideal model of water management in Central Asia and this article is an attempt to objectify this issue in international regional researches.

Water Resources of Central Asia

The region of Central Asia is situated in the centre of Eurasia and most water resources in Central Asia are transboundary water resources. There are a lot of transboundary rivers such as: Talas, Chu, Ili, Tarim, Irtysh, Tobol, Ural, but the most important for the economy of each state are Syr Darya and Amu

Darya rivers. Meanwhile, the Caspian Sea has a special role for most states because of its natural resources.

Fig 3.1: Transboundary Rivers in Central Asia

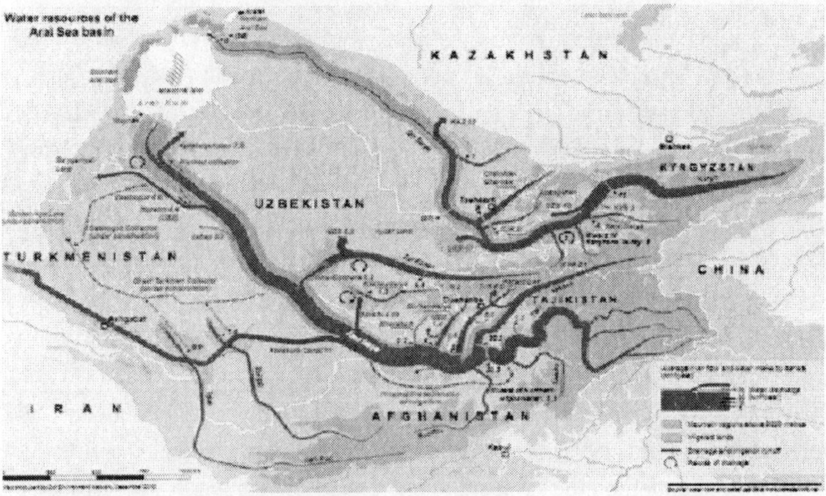

Source: http://www.cawater-info.net/aral/index_e.htm

On this map we can see basins of all the transboundary rivers of Central Asia. "Socio-economic development of the region has depended on water and land resources since time immemorial. Irrigated farming and livestock production formed the biggest part of welfare, but at the same time created vulnerable conditions and water limitations for ecosystems."[4]

Thus uneven distribution of water resources, population growth, and climate change can be a cause of future conflict in the region of Central Asia. If Central Asian states do not find solutions for their social, economic and environmental issues, they will face many problems because their economy depends on natural resources. However, we should mention that Central Asian states use some principles of international water law to protect their national interests.

Principles of International Water Law

After gaining independence, water and its legal status, taking into consideration national interests, became a significant aspect for Central Asian states. In international practice states solve problems using negotiations and treaties. However, there were some cases when states refused to cooperate and later there were interstate conflicts that reflected negatively on the environment of the region. For instance, there has been a dramatic decrease in the size of the Lake Chad over the past years. Straddling the borders of Chad, Niger and Cameroon in West Africa, Lake Chad has been a source of freshwater for irrigation projects in each of these countries. Since 1963, the lake has shrunk to nearly a twentieth of its original size, due both to climatic changes and to high demands for agricultural water. The changes in the lake have contributed to local lack of water, crop failures, livestock deaths, collapsed fisheries, soil salinity, and increasing poverty throughout the region.[5] This is a sample of uncoordinated actions that influenced the ecosystem of the region and changed the living conditions of local people.

There are now international conventions and agreements regarding international waters, which influence signatory powers. For example, Convention on Environmental Impact Assessment in a Transboundary Context (1991), Convention on the Protection and Use of Transboundary Watercourses and International Lakes (1992), Rio Declaration on Environment and Development (1992), Convention on the Protection and Use of Transboundary Watercourses and International Lakes (1992) and The Helsinki Rules on the Uses of the Waters of International Rivers (1966). All these documents provide definitions of an international river basin and a set of rules of general character.

However, there are some principles in International Water Law which governments often cite in practice. For instance *The Theory of Absolute Territorial Sovereignty* follows from the assumption that a state is the master of all persons, things, and circumstances within its territory. "Accordingly, a state may adopt any measures relating to that segment of the waters flowing on its territory and freely dispose of that resource. In so doing, a state consults and is guided only by its own national interests."[6] Some specialists call this theory Harmon Doctrine. In 1895 Judson Harmon, Attorney General of the United States, used this theory in disputes over the waters of the Rio Grande River between Mexico and the USA. The theory strongly states that "absolute sovereignty allows upstream states complete freedom of action with regard to the segment of international waters flowing within their territories, irrespective of any prejudicial effect it might have on other countries downstream. This theory is favourable to upper-basin states, and, where there are several of them, to the uppermost one."[7]

The opposite theory is the *Theory of Absolute Territorial Integrity*. "Essentially, the principle permits upper riparians to exploit the waters of a river so long as such utilisation does not affect the interests of lower riparians. In effect, lower riparian states receive a veto power or a monopoly over the water rights of upper riparian states."[8] It is obvious that this theory is the most suitable for downstream countries for protecting their rights for transboundary water.

The third principle is *Obligation Not to Cause Significant Harm.* According to this principle, "no states in an international drainage basin are allowed to use the watercourses in their territory in such a way that would cause significant harm to other basin states or to their environment, including harm to human health or safety, to the use of the waters for beneficial purposes or to the living organisms of the watercourse systems."[9]

The fourth principle is *Principle of Equitable and Reasonable Utilisation.* "This use-oriented principle is a subset of the theory of limited territorial sovereignty. It entitles each basin state to a reasonable and equitable share of water resources for beneficial uses within its own territory. Equitable and reasonable utilisation rests on a foundation of shared sovereignty and equality of rights, but it does not necessarily mean an equal share of waters."[10]

The fifth principle is a concept of *Community of Interests*. "This community of interest in a navigable river became the basis of a common legal right, the essential features of which are the perfect equality of all riparian states in the use of the whole course of the river and the exclusion of any preferential privilege of any one riparian state in relation to the others."[11]

Thus each modern state tries to solve the problem of transboundary rivers using principles of international law as an effective tool for conflict regulation. In case of Central Asia, the best variant is to create joint projects which will be mutually beneficial to all sides and will help to avoid possible social conflicts in the region. New water management can give new opportunities to the five states to improve their economy and solve regional issues. However, if the five states of Central Asia want to get the best result in their water management, they should plan their actions taking into consideration the experience of Soviet water management to avoid possible future mistakes.

Soviet Model of Water Management

Today, the difficult legacy of the Soviet era reflects on the situation in Central Asia. During the existence of the Soviet Union, the centralised authority tried to provide the whole country with the necessary amount of cotton, regardless of the environmental, social, political consequences for modern Central Asian countries, constantly increasing cotton acreage. For instance, "in 1950 there were 2.9 million irrigated hectares in Central Asia and in 1989—7.4 million irrigated hectares."[12] In the 1960s centralised government decided to divert these rivers to irrigate the desert region in order to develop agriculture rather than supply the Aral Sea. Moreover, Soviet government put up money for building dams and canals across Central Asia for irrigation and hydroelectric power stations without considering the views of the local population and the potential environmental damage. For instance, the Soviet government built Toktogul dam in Kyrgyzstan, Rogun dam on the Vakhsh river in Tajikistan, Nurek dam which is about 75 km from Rogun and other irrigation canals using water resources of Amu Darya and Syr Darya rivers.

It is worth mentioning that the Soviet government used quotas for water and there was a barter system among states. "Dams in Kyrgyzstan and Tajikistan collected and stored water in autumn and winter and released it in spring and summer to irrigate downstream crops. In exchange, Uzbekistan and Kazakhstan provided oil, coal and electricity from their thermal plants to Kyrgyzstan and Tajikistan during winter months."[13] Later, "by the mid-1990s, Kazakhstan and Uzbekistan no longer had surplus electricity to barter, so started asking market prices for their hydrocarbon exports. Kyrgyzstan and Tajikistan, unable to pay these for fuel to run their heating plants, began releasing water in winter to produce hydroelectricity to heat their own homes and factories."[14]

To sum up, Soviet water management implemented water projects only for the entire country. Later, these projects caused tension in society because newly independent states implemented their own interests in the water resources of Central Asia and they were not ready to implement new water management because they did not take into consideration the interests of each state. Soon the result of Soviet projects demonstrated environmental disaster for the whole region of Central Asia, leading to the Aral Sea crisis.

The Aral Sea Crisis

The Aral Sea is located between Kazakhstan and Uzbekistan. Many years ago, this water resource was one of the largest lakes in the world. During the Soviet period, the government decided to realise its strategic utility. The demise of the Aral Sea in Central Asia was caused primarily by the diversion of the inflowing Amu Darya and Syr Darya rivers to provide irrigation water for local croplands. These diversions dramatically reduced the river inflows, causing the Aral Sea to shrink by more than 50%, to lose two-thirds of its volume, and to greatly increase its salinity.[15] In 1963, the surface of the Aral Sea was "66,100 km^2, with an average depth of 16 m and a maximum depth of 68 m. In 1987, 27,000 km^2 of the former sea became dry land and its salt concentration had doubled."[16] In addition to this, "fishing in the Aral Sea has ceased completely, while shipping and other water-related activities have declined; the associated economic changes have taken a heavy toll on agricultural production."[17]

It is noteworthy that the "quality of drinking water continued to decline due to increasing salinity, bacteriological contamination, and the presence of pesticides and heavy metals."[18] As a result, people who live in this region suffer from anaemia, viral hepatitis, tuberculosis, typhoid fever and cancer. Public attention to the Aral issue and its impact on other countries has led to the creation of a Fund For Saving the Aral Sea. Kazakhstan, the World Bank, UNDP, UNEP, USAID, the Kuwait Fund and others financed this fund. For instance, UNICEF introduced ASPERA programme (project for environmental and regional assistance in Aral region). This programme helped mothers and children from Kazakhstan (Kyzylorda region), Turkmenistan and Uzbekistan to get immunity vaccines, medical personnel had special training courses, hospitals got medical equipment, etc. The USAID organisation also contributed to regional development.

Thus USAID funded the Environmental Policy and Technology (EPT) project in 1993-1998 and initiated a new, major effort in 2001 known as the Natural Resource Management Project (NRMP). This is a 5-year effort focusing on providing assistance to Kazakhstan, Kyrgyzstan, Turkmenistan and Uzbekistan to improve management of water, energy and land.[19] It is noteworthy that in the early 1990s, the World Bank was the first major agency which formulated an Aral Sea Basin Assistance Programme and financed "250 million US dollars, later upped to 470 million US dollars."[20] Nowadays Central Asia is a sample of how Soviet water management influenced irrigation, energy production and ecosystem of the region. We should point out that international organisations contributed towards helping people of the region. Thanks to the financial help of Central Asian countries and international donors, the part of the Aral Sea within Kazakhstan could be preserved. At present, in spite of all efforts, we can see only some species of animals in the Sea.

Water Management in the Newly Independent States

After gaining independence, the five Central Asian states declared that only joint efforts in water management and coordinated actions could help to solve the problems of the region and reduce social tension. Thus in 1992 five Central Asian states established Interstate Commission for Water Coordination of Central Asia (ICWC). ICWC Statute 4 prioritises the implementation of a regional policy of shared water use on an equitable basis, development and implementation of joint programmes for water supply improvement in the shared basins of the region.[21] The main objectives include determination of unified water policy, elaboration of its major directions with regard to population and industry branches, rational use and protection of water resources, large reservoirs regulation and river flow provision.

In 1993, these states signed another agreement about their commitment to cooperate in the management of water resources. This agreement established institutions including Interstate Council on the Aral Sea Problems, Executive Committee of ICAS, and a secretariat for ICAS and Fund for the Aral Sea. Later, member states established IFAS Executive Committee and it became a permanent body that included two representatives from each state. Despite the fact that Interstate Commission tries to solve many regional issues, there is still a long way to go towards perfect cooperation between states, because of lack of experience and various interests. However, member states do their best to solve regional water issues and maybe in future this cooperation will bring effective results for the region of Central Asia.

Sharing the Syr Darya River

A transboundary river shared by Kazakhstan, Uzbekistan and Kyrgyzstan, the Syr Darya draws upon the water sources of the Naryn river. "The Naryn originates in Kyrgyzstan, flows into Fergana Valley and becomes known as the Syr Darya after it joins the Kara Darya. It crosses Uzbek and Tajik territory before it flows again into Uzbekistan and then into Kazakhstan, where it ends in the northern part of the Aral Sea."[22] Syr Darya unites three countries with barter agreements on energy provision and water use. However, there are some problems with these agreements. For instance, according to the barter agreement between Central Asian states, Uzbekistan provided Kyrgyzstan with gas, while Kyrgyzstan supplied Uzbekistan with energy. In 2001, there were some technical problems with gas supply in Uzbekistan, because gas pipelines were in need of repair. As a result, there were no constant gas transfers from Uzbekistan to Kyrgyzstan. This case forced Kyrgyzstan to produce more electricity for their heating, using water resources from the river and it negatively influenced the irrigation projects of Uzbekistan in summer. According to specialists, "a major problem with barter agreements is that they get delayed until the late spring or early summer—the time when the downstream countries need water for irrigation."[23] Kyrgyzstan also had some problems with Kazakhstan, because both sides could not fulfil barter obligations. According to agreement, Kazakhstan sent coal to Kyrgyzstan. After the collapse of the Soviet Union, coal mines in Kazakhstan became private and it was impossible to send coal for "free" to Kyrgyzstan. There are some coal mines in Kyrgyzstan, but their quality is not good which is why Kyrgyzstan had to buy coal from Kazakhstan. Kazakhstan, in its turn, bought electricity from Kyrgyzstan, but lately, Kyrgyzstan increased prices for electricity and Kazakhstan refused to buy it.

The problem arose due to the following reason. "Kyrgyzstan tried to persuade Uzbekistan and Kazakhstan to share the costs of maintaining and operating the Toktogul Reservoir. The cost of maintaining and operating the reservoir is estimated at between US $15 million and US $27 million per year—a price Kyrgyzstan is not willing or able to pay."[24] Kazakhstan and Uzbekistan did not accept this law and refused to pay this sum of money to Kyrgyzstan. Lately, Kyrgyzstan changed its position and "insisted on only sharing maintenance costs. Kazakhstan agreed to share these costs; meanwhile, Uzbekistan agreed to cover some costs in return for a guarantee that it would receive water for irrigation."[25] Kyrgyzstan, in its turn, "indicated willingness to cease production of electricity at Toktogul during winter if Uzbekistan and Kazakhstan compensated it for its losses."[26] Thus these barter agreements demonstrated their inefficiency for the economy of Central Asian states, because all signatories could not fulfil their obligations on time. Moreover, Soviet specialists diverted the river to different areas and when Kyrgyzstan needs more electricity in winter, they release water from Toktogul reservoir. As a result, downstream countries Kazakhstan and Uzbekistan experience floods in winter.

It is notable that present relations between Kazakhstan and Kyrgyzstan differ from the past. Recently, both sides decided to tackle energy issues and there were some meetings in Kazakhstan. For instance, "November 7, 2014 there was an official visit of the President of Kyrgyzstan Almazbek Atambayev to Kazakhstan. Both sides discussed their cooperation in trade, economy, investments, energy, logistics, transport, culture and other spheres."[27] It is remarkable that countries of Central Asia are ready for a dialogue and cooperation in different spheres. If these states want to change the situation, they should find new approaches and sign new effective treaties which will take into consideration the interests of all sides.

Dividing the Amu Darya

The Amu Darya is the largest river in the region of Central Asia. It is a transboundary river for Tajikistan, Kyrgyzstan, Afghanistan, Turkmenistan and Uzbekistan. Most of the river flows "on the territory of Tajikistan (72.8%), 14.6% in Afghanistan and 8.5% in Uzbekistan. Three major tributaries contribute to the river: Kafirnigan, Sherabad and Surhandarya."[28] According to water quotas, Turkmenistan and Uzbekistan divide Amu Darya equally, however, according to the Uzbek side, Uzbekistan needs more water because of irrigation and population growth. The main concern for Uzbekistan is the fact that in 2000 Turkmenistan began to create an artificial lake called The Golden Century Lake. This artificial lake takes water resources from Amu Darya and it is evident that if the Turkmen side takes too much water, it will negatively influence the irrigation plans of Uzbekistan. Moreover, "environmentalists say that a lot of the water will simply disappear into the desert's permeable soil. Large amounts will also evaporate in the high temperatures, leaving the soil extremely salty."[29] If this happens, it will be an environmental disaster for the whole region and will cause social tension among neighbours.Thus the absence of a new treaty and realisation of new water projects can be a reason for future destabilisation in the region of Central Asia.

The internal problem of Uzbekistan with water delimitation among three provinces also can worsen the situation. The problem is that Navoi, Bukhara and Surkhandarya provinces take more water, while other provinces of Uzbekistan get less water. All this leads to the fact that water resources in case of population growth and unequal distribution can threaten the stability of the region. If Central Asian states cooperate or develop alternative sources then there will be less pressure on water resources and it will help to regulate disputes. Similarly, Uzbekistan has unresolved issues with Tajikistan. According to swap agreement, Tajikistan exported hydroelectric power to Uzbekistan, and in exchange, Uzbekistan sent gas to Tajikistan. After some time, Uzbekistan could not supply gas to Tajikistan on a temporary basis because of technical problems. So, Tajikistan also had lack of electricity and decided to construct additional dams for internal supply. Tajikistan has Nurek dam and hydropower station on its territory; however, according to the Tajik government there is need to generate more electricity for their internal demand and for budget replenishment.

The Soviet government constructed Nurek dam between 1961 and 1980 along the Vakhsh river in Tajikistan. In 1967 the Soviet government decided to build Rogun dam, but did not finish this project because of the disintegration of the Soviet Union. At present, Tajikistan plans to complete the construction of Rogun dam with foreign investments. Referring to the data of "Barki Tojik, Tajikistan invested US $1 billion 200 million in energy projects during 15 years. Recently, Asian Development Bank, German Development bank, Chinese Exim Bank and Barki Tojik invested in 15 energy projects. Russia invested US $250 million for 'Sangtuda-1' project."[30] Thus Tajikistan has sought to find its own solution to the energy problems. However, these energy projects can reduce the flow of Amu Darya for irrigation, negatively influencing the ecosystem of the whole region and raising social tension.

According to the World Bank draft of Rogun project, "the dam is the best way to end the country's crippling energy shortages."[31] However, other experts have some doubts. For instance, "in a second report, Human Rights Watch says the resettlement of 42,000 people whose homes will be destroyed or flooded by Rogun is not going as smoothly as the government has promised."[32] All this leads to the conclusion that barter agreements were not effective for Central Asian states because none of the countries could fulfil its obligations. It enables us to conclude that construction of dams, population growth, unfriendly relations between states, weak economy and absence of new effective treaties influence and increase the potential for social conflicts in Central Asia. However, according to the recent researches of experts, water wastage in Central Asia is also a reason for social tension.

Conflicts Between Neighbouring States

Nowadays, many disputes in Central Asia have a complex nature. These disputes are associated with division of transboundary rivers and border delimitation, where water resources serve as a lever of pressure on a neighbouring state.

One of such samples is a case between residents of Kazakhstan and Kyrgyzstan on July 7, 2013.

> … Some 50 or 60 inhabitants of the village of Kok-Say in north-western Kyrgyzstan's Talas Region stopped the flow of water on July 7, demanding that a 2,600-hectare parcel of land ceded to Kazakhstan in a border agreement back in 2001 be returned to Kyrgyzstan (which was allocated a different plot of land the same size in exchange). With several villages in Zhambyl Region in south-eastern Kazakhstan cut off from water and farmers unable to irrigate some 4,000 hectares of land, the governments stepped in. Astana urged Bishkek to act fast to restore the flow, and "not permit such unilateral actions in future … "[33]

In this situation, the Kazakh embassy in Kyrgyzstan reported that "The illegal activity which contradicts the earlier agreements on transboundary water resources and common norms of international law provoked a lack of water not only in Kazakh Zhambyl region's Zhualynskiy area but also in the Kyrgyz villages located lower near the channel."[34] Moreover, the Kazakh embassy highlighted that "… the situation at the interstate water channel 'Bystrotok' contradicts the atmosphere of the Eternal Friendship Treaty from April 8, 1997 and the Treaty on Alliance Relations from December 25, 2003 between Kazakhstan and Kyrgyzstan."[35] Finally, both sides solved this problem after negotiations and water flow was restored on July 17. "Meanwhile Kazakhstan allowed Kyrgyz farmers to graze cattle on its territory near the channel."[36]

It is noteworthy that in spite of the fact that both sides could solve this issue, these actions affected the relations of the border population. From this event we can sum up that in spite of the signed Treaty of Friendship between the two countries, some representatives of the Kyrgyz side had raised the issue of border delimitation where the Kyrgyz side used transboundary water resources as a tool of pressure on the Kazakh side to promote its own interests without taking into consideration all official agreements on border delimitation. It should be noted that this event has a local nature which demonstrates the behaviour of some individuals living in the border areas of Kyrgyzstan and some "unscrupulous" politicians and public figures who tried to use this case for their own group interests that actually do not reflect the official political course of the state.

The following case is of a local conflict between neighbouring states that took place on the Kazakh-Uzbek border. According to Tengri News "two Kazakh men were fishing in the middle of Syr Darya when Uzbek border guards fired on them. The Uzbeks say the men were illegally crossing the border. Kazakhstan has sent a note to Uzbekistan protesting the incident. The Syr Darya does not really serve as a border between the two—except near the Shardara Reservoir in the Southern Kazakhstan Region near Uzbekistan's fertile cotton core."[37] "The survivor recalls that Uzbek border guards opened fire in their direction without any warning. The preliminary information available indicates that ten shots were fired … Uzbek special services claim that the fishermen illegally crossed the border and were fishing in foreign territory. But the survivor assures us that they sailed no more than ten metres away from the coast and could not have reached foreign territory."[38]

The Kazakh side expressed its position on the murder of a Kazakh citizen and had sent a protest note to Uzbekistan. As a result, Uzbekistan admitted the fact of use of firearms and each guilty Uzbek citizen paid a fine of 4,955 tenge ($26). It is noteworthy that signed agreements, such as Agreement of Eternal friendship (October 31, 1998), Agreement on Strategic Partnership (June 14, 2013) and Agreement on the Activity of Border Representatives (December 13, 2000) cannot guarantee safety to local people. According to this information, we can conclude that the fishery on a transboundary river is unsafe for Kazakhstan citizens because the Uzbek border guards use firearms against peaceful citizens of neighbouring states. Moreover, the impossibility of dividing a transboundary river may be the cause of similar cases in the future because fishing is the major source of income for people who live near the Kazakh-Uzbek border and there is no guarantee that fishing on the Kazakh side of the river is safe for Kazakh citizens.

Analysing issues of water resources, we should also mention that Kazakhstan has transboundary rivers with China and there are some problems between the two states. For instance, a case with Irtysh river which starts in China and then flows to Kazakhstan and Russia.

> The Irtysh river is 4,248 km long, it is one the main feeders of the Ob river (in Russia). Irtysh flows across Kazakhstan (1,700 km) and China (525

> km) ... Water from Irtysh feeds Irtysh-Karaganda channel that is used for general consumption and irrigation purposes in Kazakhstan. And there is a chain of hydropower plants on the Irtysh river below Zaissan lake. The complex includes Bukhtarma, Ust-Kamenogorsk and Shulba hydropower plants in Kazakhstan.[39]

The problem is that China uses Irtysh water for its Xinjiang Uyghur Autonomous Region without taking into consideration Kazakhstan's and Russia's interests. According to experts, "in 1999-2005 it consumed 11.4 per cent of the river's stock whereas in 2010-2011 it was consuming over 30 per cent ... Experts believe that with this rate of consumption the river will be stressed and several regions will face the severe water shortage."[40]

According to specialists, "lowering the transborder flows of the Ili and Irtysh rivers may cause depletion of the unique lakes Balkhash and Zaissan and extinction of forests in Ile-Alatau national park, Dzungarian Alatau and Tarbagatay."[41] Moreover, the specialists say that "if Balkhash repeats the sad story of the Aral Sea, a real threat will be hanging over Almaty and its citizens. Thousands of tons of salt will be picked up by wind from the drained bottom of the lake and will be carried to Almaty and eastern Kazakhstan. Salt winds may cause melting of almost 95 per cent of all the glaciers near Almaty and the whole Alatau. It is likely that the melting-waters streaming down the mountains will simply wash Almaty away in a mud-flood."[42]

It is worth mentioning that according to the data of Khanty-Mansiysk Centre of Hydrometeorology and Environmental Monitoring, there was a dramatic decrease of water flow in Ob and Irtysh rivers during 17 August -September 2, 2015. For instance, "water in Khanty-Mansiysk (Irtysh), reduced to 2 m 97 cm;

- Belogorye – 756 cm – 3m 09 cm;
- Polnovat – 858 cm – 94 cm;
- Berezovo – 666 cm – 92 cm."[43]

On the basis of this information, it can be suggested that China blocks more water on its territory to realise its own projects and none of the neighbouring states can change this situation because China did not sign the 1992 and 1993 Helsinki agreement on transboundary rivers. It is to be noted that Kazakhstan had several meetings with the Chinese delegation on the issue of transboundary water resources. Also, both sides signed a variety of agreements, had several negotiations, created a Joint Commission, however, the Chinese side did not change its plans on water and energy projects and there is still no agreement which defines the exact amount of water flow in transboundary rivers. To sum up, we can say that it is very difficult for Kazakhstan to persuade China to sign international treaties on transboundary rivers and agreements on water division because China prefers only bilateral negotiations and refers to the work of the Joint Commission in water issues.

Finally it can be observed that such issues as: border delimitation and demarcation, economic development of cross-border water resources and management of transboundary water resources have a conflict potential in their nature, as we notice in the above-mentioned information. Searching for the origins of the problems and their solution in the international legal framework is the basis of harmonious and peaceful social development in Central Asia.

Central Asian States Are Water Wasters

While most reports state that there is a water shortage in Central Asia, a recent research of Finnish expert Olli Varis proved the opposite. According to his report, water wastage in Central Asia is the main problem of the region. The scientist published a report, and proved that there is no shortage of water in Central Asia. "These countries have plenty of water for their populations. The annual availability of fresh water per capita for the Amu Darya (2,087 cubic metres) and the Syr Darya (1,744 m^3) river basins are well above the United Nations definitions of water shortages: 1,000 m^3 per capita constitutes a chronic shortage, and 1,700 m^3 a moderate shortage. By comparison, Denmark has 1,128 m^3 of water per capita, Germany 1,878 m^3 and the United Kingdom 2,465 m^3."[44]

Olli Varis listed the highest average per capita users of water in the world.

Fig 3.2: Top 20 Consumers

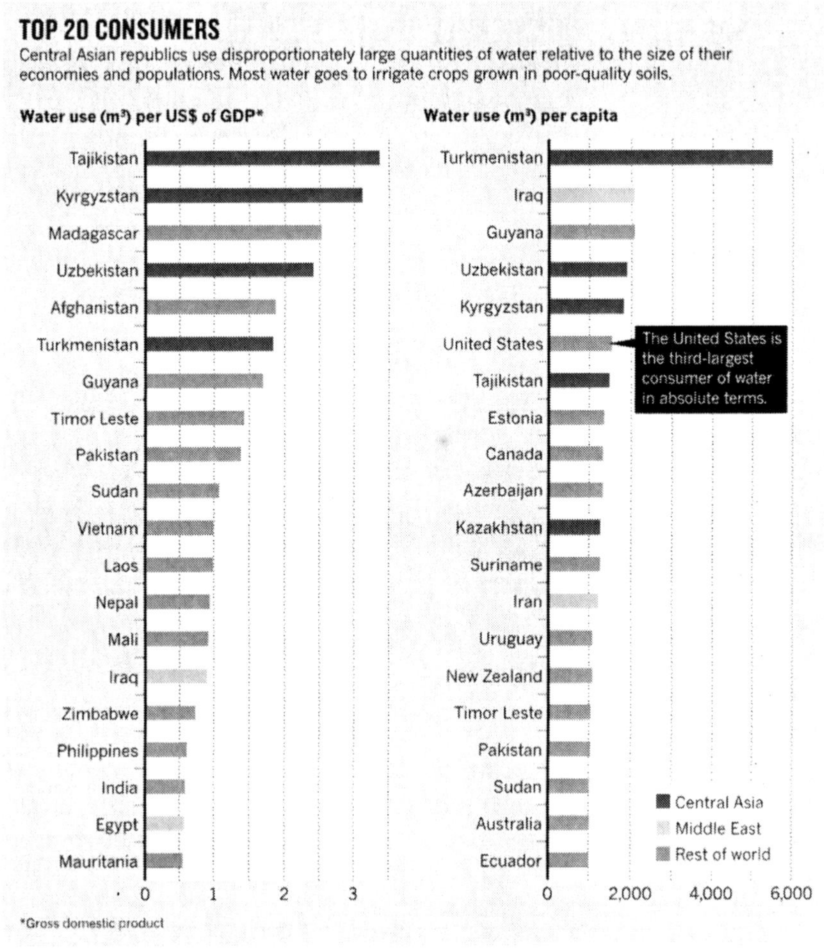

Source: http://www.nature.com/news/resources-curb-vast-water-use-in-central-asia-.16017 [45] (December 30, 2014).

According to this table, we can notice that Turkmenistan is the leader in water use per capita. This country uses approximately 5,500 cubic metres of water. We can also see that Uzbekistan comes in 4th and Kazakhstan in 11th in this ranking of top consumers. This leads to the conclusion that old irrigation system causes water wastage and if states do not change it, they will lose water annually. The problem about decrease in water is hardly taken into consideration. Varis opines that "… economic growth is dominated by the oil and gas industry and by urban expansion. Already, more than half of the region's population is urban and that proportion is rising. Despite this, Central Asian economies continue to focus on primary industries such as agriculture and the extraction of fossil fuels."[46] States should develop cooperation in water management, however, this presents difficulties for all riparians.

Complexities for Future Cooperation

A number of researches have demonstrated the complexities of cooperation among riparian states in the world. Many scientists explain different reasons for this uneasiness, for example, according to Asit K. Biswas,

> … national sovereignty is the most important political consideration at the nation-state levels. Historically, all the nation-states have jealously guarded their sovereign powers to manage the activities within their own borders. Thus not surprisingly, the overall discussions on the management of transboundary rivers and lakes have often been somewhat controversial because of consideration of national sovereignty issues.[47]

As a sample, Biswas talks about the Conference on the Human Environment, held in Stockholm in 1972 when Brazil showed its position towards management of shared natural resources. In addition, he writes that "the second reason is the perceived national self-interests of the various co-riparians on the numerous transboundary rivers and lakes on which operational treaties do not exist at present."[48] Biswas points to the fact that countries which are currently negotiating treaties on transboundary rivers with their co-basin counterparts, or likely to do so in the foreseeable future, often feel that they would prefer to resolve the problems on the basis of bilateral or multilateral negotiations, rather than through an intermediary international or foreign institution. The countries generally prefer not to be constrained by international norms or guidelines, which, they fear, might reduce their ability to manouvre. Accordingly, they often either take a strong stand against such norms or abstain from the discussion or voting. Behind the scenes, however, many countries have often let their views known to the staff members of the international organisations in no uncertain terms: they would prefer them to stay away.[49]

To conclude, it is evident that national sovereignty and perceived national self-interests influence the signing of trans-border agreements. In the Central

Asian case, there are some complexities which have a negative influence on cooperation. For instance, according to Erika Weinthal, "the clash between upstream and midstream interests for agriculture and the downstream interests for clean potable water represented a situation in which the disincentives for cooperation were starkest."[50] Weinthal demonstrates a table of potential water-related conflicts in the Aral basin, taking into consideration the nature of the conflicts, potential conflicts and states that share the basin.

Table 3.1: Potential Water-Related Conflicts in the Aral Basin

Drainage basin	States that share basin	Potential conflicts	Nature of conflict
Syr Darya	Kyrgyzstan (upstream), Uzbekistan (midstream), Tajikistan (midstream), Kazakhstan (downstream)	Among Kyrgyzstan, Uzbekistan, and Kazakhstan over water releases from Toktogul Reservoir	Energy vs. irrigation
		Between upstream agricultural users in Fergana Valley and Golodnaya Steppe and downstream users in Kazakhstan	Quantity and quality of water; agriculture vs. potable water
Amu Darya	Tajikistan (upstream), Uzbekistan (midstream), Turkmenistan (downstream), Karakalpakstan in Uzbekistan (downstream)	Between Turkmenistan and Uzbekistan in regard to water withdrawals from Kara Kum Canal	Quantity
		Other potential conflicts over water sharing in lower Amu Darya between Uzbekistan and Turkmenistan	Quantity
		Between upstream users in Tajikistan and downstream users in Turkmenistan, Uzbekistan, and Karakalpakstan	Quantity and quality; long-term potential conflict between energy vs. irrigation
Zarafshon	Tajikistan (upstream), Uzbekistan (downstream)	Between upstream users in Tajikistan and downstream users in Uzbekistan	Quantity

Source: Erika Weinthal, "State making and environmental cooperation: linking domestic and international politics in Central Asia," p. 120.[51]

This table clearly indicates that energy, irrigation, quantity and quality of water are the main reasons for potential conflict among riparians. We can conclude that old barter agreements, water storage and uncoordinated energy projects using water of transboundary rivers worsened the economy of some Central Asia states. Unless the region's economy depends on natural resources, there is a risk of social conflict, however, if Central Asian states cooperate, they can decide many regional problems and improve their economy.

Recommendations for Central Asian States

- States should realise coordinated foreign policy with priority on regional integration, trying to find a balance and compromise between national and regional interests;

- Socio-economic integration can help to solve many issues of the region. It is necessary to increase joint economic projects (agriculture, energy, environmental policy, joint investment projects), considering the interests of all sides;
- Five Central Asian states should finance joint regional projects without external funding to escape possible imbalance between states. Also, the states should create a financial mechanism for financing relevant regional projects;
- Central Asian states should implement innovations to save water in different spheres. Moreover, they can create a joint regional innovation bank in the spheres of energy, agriculture, environment, transport, logistics and social projects;
- States need specialists who have excellent knowledge of water management, international water law, international relations, negotiation strategy and management of human resources;
- States should use international experience in their water management of transboundary waters;
- States should solve issues of their borders and make "controversial" areas free economic zones in Central Asia, with the prospect of future transformation of the whole region as a free economic zone;
- States should develop economic integration processes to improve their economy and social conditions.

Notes

1. Ardalyon Kibanov, Ivan Vorozheikin and Valeria Konovalova, *Theory of a conflict* (Moscow: Infra-M, 2011), p. 288.
2. Eduard Utkin, *Conflictology: Theory and practice* (Moscow: Ekmos, 2000), p. 53.
3. Gennadii Kozyrev, *Introduction to the Conflictology* (Moscow: Vlados, 2001), p. 6.
4. "Central Asia: background information," *Interstate Commission for Water Coordination,* 2014, accessed October 16, 2014, http://www.icwc-aral.uz/general.htm
5. "Lake Chad: almost gone," UNEP, 2014, accessed December 20, 2014, http://www.unep.org/dewa/vitalwater/article116.html
6. Takele Soboka Bulto, "Between Ambivalence and Necessity: Occlusions on the Path Toward a Basin-Wide Treaty in the Nile Basin," *Colorado Journal of International Environmental Law and Policy*, vol. 20, 2009, p. 302, accessed December 30, 2014, http://www.colorado.edu/law/sites/default/files/Vol.20.3.pdf
7. Bulto, "Between Ambivalence and Necessity," p. 303.
8. Gabriel Eckstein, "Application of International Water Law to transboundary Groundwater Resources, and the Slovak-Hungarian Dispute over Gabcikovo-Nagymaros," *Suffolk Transnational Law Review,* vol. 19, 1995, accessed December 30,

2014, http://www.internationalwaterlaw.org/bibliography/articles/transboundarygw.html#N_17_

9. Muhammad Mizanur Rahaman, "Principles of Transboundary Water Resources Management and Ganges Treaties: An Analysis," *Water Resources Development*, vol. 25, no. 1, 2009, p. 162, accessed December 30, 2014, http://www.internationalwaterlaw.org/bibliography/articles/general/Rahaman-Ganges-Water_Res_Devel.pdf
10. Rahaman, "Principles of Transboundary Water Resources Management," p. 160.
11. *Publications of the permanent court of international justice,* Series A, no. 23, Case relating to the territorial jurisdiction of the international commission of the river order, series A, no. 23, no. 16, 1929, p. 27, accessed December 30, 2014, http://www.icj-cij.org/pcij/serie_A/A_23/74_Commission_internationale_de_l_Oder_Arret.pdf
12. Beate Ashment, "Water resources distribution in Central Asia: an insoluble problem," Friedrich Ebert Foundation, May, 2011, accessed December 30, 2014, http://library.fes.de/pdf-files/bueros/moskau/08598.pdf
13. ICG, "Water pressures in Central Asia," 3, No. 233, accessed September 11, 2014, http://www.crisisgroup.org/~/media/Files/europe/central-asia/233-water-pressures-in-central-asia.pdf
14. "Water pressures in Central Asia."
15. "The disappearance of the Aral Sea," *Vital Water Graphics*, 2008, accessed December 30, 2014, http://www.unep.org/dewa/vitalwater/article115.html
16. "The disappearance of the Aral Sea."
17. "The disappearance of the Aral Sea."
18. "The disappearance of the Aral Sea."
19. Gulnara Roll, Natalia Alexeeva et al., "Aral Sea experience and lessons learned brief," accessed December 30, 2014, http://www.worldlakes.org/uploads/01_Aral_Sea_27February2006.pdf
20. "Aral Sea experience and lessons learned brief," p. 9.
21. Statute 4, "Statute of the Interstate Commission for Water Coordination of Central Asia," ICWC, http://icwc-aral.uz/statute4. htm ;
22. "The Amu Darya and the Syr Darya, Central Asia's lifelines," accessed December 30, 2014, http://www.waterunites-ca.org/themes.html?view=booktext&id=29&tmpl=component
23. "Central Asia: Water and conflict," ICG, no. 34, May 2002, accessed December 30, 2014. http://www.crisisgroup.org/~/media/Files/asia/central-asia/Central%20Asia%20Water%20and%20Conflict.pdf
24. "Central Asia: Water and conflict," p. 15.
25. "Central Asia: Water and conflict."
26. "Central Asia: Water and conflict."
27. "Almazbek Atambayev President of Kyrgyzstan visited Kazakhstan," Akorda, 2014, accessed December 30, 2014. http://akorda.kz/ru/page/page_218302_vstrecha-s-prezidentom-kyrgyzskoi-respubliki-almazbekom-atambaevym-pribyvshim-v-kazakhstan-s-gosudar
28. "Amu Darya river basin." Amu Darya basin network, accessed December 30, 2014, http://amudaryabasin.net/content/amu-darya-river-basin
29. "Turkmenistan to create desert sea," BBC news, July 16, 2009, accessed December 30, 2014, http://news.bbc.co.uk/2/hi/asia-pacific/8154467.stm
30. Farkhod Milod, Holikzod Mirzonabi, "Whom to trust the construction of hydroelectric

power station in Tajikistan: Russia or China," *Centrasia*, September 2014, accessed December 30, 2014, http://www.centrasia.ru/newsA.php?st=1409809740

31. David Trilling, "Tajikistan: World Bank Gives Dam Green Light; Rights Watchdog Worried," Eurasianey.org, 2014, accessed December 30, 2014, http://www.eurasianet.org/node/68761
32. "Tajikistan: World Bank Gives Dam Green Light."
33. Joanna Lillis, "Kyrgyzstan and Kazakhstan: water dispute highlights potential for conflict," July 18, 2013, accessed August 28, 2015, http://www.eurasianet.org/node/67267
34. "Kazakhstan appealed to Kyrgyzstan over transboundary water resources," July 16, 2013, accessed August 28, 2015, http://www.azernews.az/region/56922.html
35. "Kazakhstan appealed to Kyrgyzstan over transboundary water resources."
36. "Kazakhstan and Kyrgyzstan negotiates on Bystrotok interstate channel," July 22, 2013, accessed August 28, 2015, http://bnews.kz/en/news/post/149909/
37. Catherine Putz, "Kazakh fisherman shot by Uzbek border guards," July 2, 2015, accessed August 28, 2015, http://thediplomat.com/2015/07/kazakh-fisherman-shot-by-uzbek-border-guards/
38. Interfax, "Uzbek border guards shot Kazakh fisherman dead—media," June 30, 2015, accessed August 28, 2015, http://www.interfax.com/newsinf.asp?id=602582
39. Tengri News, "Irtysh river problems may cause water shortages in Kazakhstan and Russia," September 10, 2010, accessed August 28, 2015, http://en.tengrinews.kz/environment/Irtysh-River-problems-may-cause-water-shortages-in-22014/
40. Tengri News, "Irtysh river problems may cause water shortages in Kazakhstan and Russia," September 10, 2013, accessed August 28, 2015, http://en.tengrinews.kz/environment/Irtysh-River-problems-may-cause-water-shortages-in-22014/
41. "China may turn Kazakhstan into desert," January 25, 2013, accessed August 28, 2015, https://uyghuramerican.org/article/china-may-turn-kazakhstan-desert.html
42. "China may turn Kazakhstan into desert."
43. http://www.ugrapro.ru/2015/09/02/za-16-dney-v-rekah-irtyish-voda-upala-na-2-97-sm-a-na-obi-3-09sm/. Accessed August 28,2015,
44. Olli Varis, "Resources: Curb vast water use in Central Asia," *Nature*, October 1, 2014, http://www.nature.com/news/resources-curb-vast-water-use-in-central-asia-1.16017
45. "Resources: Curb vast water use in Central Asia."
46. "Resources: Curb vast water use in Central Asia."
47. Asit K. Biswas, "Management of Transboundary waters: An Overview," in Olli Varis, Cecilia Tortajada and Asit K. Biswas (eds.), *Management of transboundary rivers and lakes* (Springer-Verlag Berlin Heidelberg, 2008): 8-9.
48. "Management of Transboundary waters: An Overview."
49. "Management of Transboundary waters: An Overview."
50. Erika Weinthal, "The need for aid: failed reform, potential conflict, and legacy of cotton monoculture," in Erika Weinthal (ed.), *State making and environmental cooperation linking domestic and international politics in Central Asia* (Cambridge, Massachusetts: The MIT Press, 2002), p. 120.
51. Weinthal, "The need for aid."

Bibliography

Akorda. "Almazbek Atambayev President of Kyrgyzstan visited Kazakhstan." Akorda. 2014. Accessed December 30, 2014. http://akorda.kz/ru/page/page_218302_vstrecha-s-prezidentom-kyrgyzskoi-respubliki-almazbekom-atambaevym-pribyvshim-v-kazakhstan-s-gosudar.

Amu Darya basin network. "Amu Darya river basin." Amu Darya basin network. 2014. Accessed December 30, 2014, http://amudaryabasin.net/content/amu-darya-river-basin.

Ashment, Beate. "Water resources distribution in Central Asia: an insoluble problem." *Friedrich Ebert Foundation*. 2011. Accessed December 30, 2014. http://library.fes.de/pdf-files/bueros/moskau/08598.pdf.

Azernews. "Kazakhstan appealed to Kyrgyzstan over transboundary water resources." Azernews. Accessed August 28 2015. http://www.azernews.az/region/56922.html.

BBC. "Turkmenistan to create desert sea." BBC. 2009. Accessed July 16, 2014. http://news.bbc.co.uk/2/hi/asia-pacific/8154467.stm.

Biswas, Asit K. "Management of Transboundary waters: An Overview." In *Management of transboundary rivers and lakes*, edited by Olli Varis, Cecilia Tortajada and Asit K. Biswas, 8-9. Springer-Verlag Berlin Heidelberg, 2008.

BNews.kz. "Kazakhstan and Kyrgyzstan negotiates on Bystrotok interstate channel." Accessed August 28, 2015. http://bnews.kz/en/news/post/149909/.

Bulto, Takele Soboka. "Between Ambivalence and Necessity: Occlusions on the Path Toward a Basin-Wide Treaty in the Nile Basin." In *Colorado Journal of International Environmental Law and Policy* 302, vol. 20 (2009). Accessed December 30, 2014. http://www.colorado.edu/law/sites/default/files/Vol.20.3.pdf.

CAWATERinfo. "The Aral sea." CAWATERinfo. 2014. Accessed October 16, 2014. http://www.cawater-info.net/aral/index_e.htm.

Eckstein, Gabriel. "Application of International Water Law to transboundary Groundwater Resources, and the Slovak-Hungarian Dispute over Gabcikovo-Nagymaros." *Suffolk Transnational Law Review*, vol. 19 (1995). Accessed December 30 2014. http://www.internationalwaterlaw.org/bibliography/articles/transboundarygw.html#N_17_.

ICG. "Central Asia: Water and conflict" *ICG*, no. 34 (2002). Accessed December 30, 2014. http://www.crisisgroup.org/~/media/Files/asia/central-asia/Central%20Asia%20Water%20and%20Conflict.pdf.

ICG. "Water pressures in Central Asia." *ICG*, no. 233 (2014). Accessed September 11, 2014. http://www.crisisgroup.org/~/media/Files/europe/central-asia/233-water-pressures-in-central-asia.pdf.

ICWC. "Statute of the Interstate Commission for Water Coordination of Central Asia." ICWC. Accessed December 30, 2014. http://icwc-aral.uz/statute4.htm.

ICWC. "Central Asia: background information." ICWC. Accessed October 16, 2014. http://www.icwc-aral.uz/general.htm.

Interfax. "Uzbek border guards shot Kazakh fisherman dead—media." Interfax. Accessed August 28, 2015. http://www.interfax.com/newsinf.asp?id=602582.

Kibanov, Ardalyon, Ivan Vorozheikin and Valeria Konovalova. *Theory of a conflict*. Moscow: Infra-M, 2011: 288.

Kozyrev, Gennadii. *Introduction to the Conflictology*. Moscow: Vlados, 2001:6.

Lillis, Joanna. "Kyrgyzstan and Kazakhstan: water dispute highlights potential for conflict." Accessed August 2, 2015. http://www.eurasianet.org/node/67267.

Milod, Farkhod and Mirzonabi Holikzod. "Whom to trust the construction of hydroelectric power station in Tajikistan: Russia or China." *Centrasia*. Accessed September 2014. http://www.centrasia.ru/newsA.php?st=1409809740.

Publications of the Permanent Court of International Justice. Series A, no. 23. "Case relating to the territorial, jurisdiction of the international commission of the river order," series A, no. 23, no. 16 (1929). Accessed December 30, 2014. http://www.icj-cij.org/pcij/serie_A/A_23/74_Commission_internationale_de_l_Oder_Arret.pdf.

Putz, Catherine. "Kazakh fisherman shot by Uzbek border guards." Accessed August 28, 2015, http://thediplomat.com/2015/07/kazakh-fisherman-shot-by-uzbek-border-guards/.

Rahaman, Muhammad Mizanur. "Principles of Transboundary Water Resources Management and Ganges Treaties: An Analysis." *Water Resources Development*, vol. 25, no. 1 (2009). Accessed December 30, 2014. 162. http://www.internationalwaterlaw.org/bibliography/articles/general/Rahaman-Ganges-Water_Res_Devel.pdf.

Roll, Gulnara and Natalia Alexeeva et al. "Aral Sea experience and lessons learned brief." Accessed December 30, 2014.http://www.worldlakes.org/uploads/01_Aral_Sea_27February2006.pdf.

Tengri News. "Irtysh river problems may cause water shortages in Kazakhstan and Russia." Tengri News. September 10, 2010. Accessed August 28, 2015. http://en.tengrinews.kz/environment/Irtysh-River-problems-may-cause-water-shortages-in-22014/.

Trilling, David. "Tajikistan: World Bank Gives Dam Green Light; Rights Watchdog Worried." *Eurasianet.org*. 2014. Accessed December 30, 2014.http://www.eurasianet.org/node/68761.

UgraPro. http://www.ugrapro.ru/2015/09/02/za-16-dney-v-rekah-irtyish-voda-upala-na-2-97-sm-a-na-obi-3-09sm/

UNEP. "Lake Chad: almost gone." *UNEP*. 2014. Accessed December 20, 2014. http://www.unep.org/dewa/vitalwater/article116.html.

Uyghur American Association. "China may turn Kazakhstan into desert." Uyghur American Association. Accessed August 28, 2015. https://uyghuramerican.org/article/china-may-turn-kazakhstan-desert.html.

Utkin, Eduard. *Conflictology: Theory and Practice.* Moscow: Ekmos, 2000.

Varis, Olli. "Resources: Curb vast water use in Central Asia." *Nature* (2014). Accessed October 1, 2014. http://www.nature.com/news/resources-curb-vast-water-use-in-central-asia-1.16017.

Vital water graphics. "The disappearance of the Aral Sea." *Vital Water Graphics*. 2008. Accessed December, 30, 2014.
http://www.unep.org/dewa/vitalwater/article115.html.

Water Unites. "The Amu Darya and the Syr Darya, Central Asia's lifelines." *Water Unites*. 2014. Accessed December 30, 2014. http://www.waterunites-ca.org/themes.html?view=booktext&id=29&tmpl=component.

Weinthal, Erika. "The need for aid: failed reform, potential conflict, and legacy of cotton monoculture." In *State making and environmental cooperation linking domestic and international politics in Central Asia*, edited by Erika Weinthal, 120. Cambridge, Massachusetts: The MIT Press, 2002.

Moments, Imaginings and Movements

4. Exploring the Symbolic Dimension of Social Protest: An Analysis of Public Representations of Opposition to Putin's Regime During the Moscow Protest Campaign of 2011-2012

Olga Malinova

The protest campaign against "the unfair elections" in Russia that took place in the winter of 2011-2012 was largely unexpected. In the assessment of sociologists, the level of dissatisfaction with the government "was not critical," besides it was unevenly distributed—economic dissatisfaction was concentrated in large regional cities, while political discontent was more typical for capital cities and megapolises.[1] In the previous years the ruling regime developed a sophisticated institutional infrastructure to keep public opposition under control.[2] Before winter 2011, protest actions focused on political issues were not popular; oppositional political parties and formally established NGOs played a major role in their organisation.[3] So, when in December 2011 a spontaneous protest rally campaign against the fraud at the State Duma election started in Moscow and some large cities, it brought before social scientists a number of questions. Taking into account that suspicion concerning a fraud accompanied the Russian elections since the mid-1990s, it was not clear why at this time it caused such negative public reaction. Who were the "new" protesters—"the angry city dwellers" (*rasserzhennyegorozhane*), as they were termed in newspapers? Why was it that the winter rally campaign could unite the political forces that had never been allies before—the Liberals, the Russian nationalists, various civic non-political organisations, and "independent" individuals? How could it happen that even with a lack of established leaders and clear programme, the protest movement lasted till June of 2012 and recruited new participants? Finally, what were the most important factors of its subsequent decline? It must be confirmed that social scientists were fully equipped to study the "unexpected protest": starting with the second large meeting in Moscow at Sakharov Avenue on December 24 there were pollsters from Levada Centre and VCIOM, besides there were numerous field research initiatives of sociologists, anthropologists and political scientists who collected verbal and visual material often making it available to the other researchers via thematic groups on Facebook and websites. Owing to this quick reaction now we have a large bulk of material for study of the protest campaign of 2011-2012, mostly for Moscow, but also for St. Petersburg and some regional cities.

It is not surprising that soon after the events a wave of research publications appeared in Russia and abroad. Scholars give different explanations about the rise and subsequent failure of "unexpected protest." Many of them connect it to "attitude changes and shifts in the social structure, such as the emergence of a mass urban middle class,"[4] that was fostered by economic growth in the 2000s. Even if the connection between the protest against unfair elections and rise of the new social groups is not that straightforward,[5] still it is a fact that according to surveys the majority of the protesters could be ascribed to "the marginal middle class," i.e., to the educated groups with relatively high level of income and specific patterns of consumption that consist mostly of employees.[6] Some researchers also explain the new patterns of protest behaviour by wider participation of the younger people who had no previous experience of mass actions, but had skills of online communication.[7] By analogy "Facebook revolutions" in the Middle East, the new communication technologies, and in particular the spread of Internet access in Russia and widening involvement in the social networks are considered the second reason for the rise of protest activity. Finally, some scholars relate the wave of protest activity to inherent drawbacks of Putin's regime of "managed democracy" that could not answer to "the very diversity of the new era of contentious politics" that "has generated political pluralism in society."[8] Each of these explanations gives an important piece of the puzzle. However, according to my argument, to arrange them into a comprehensive picture we also need to look more systematically at the symbolic dimension of the protest movement that helps to explain it as a dynamic process of development and subsequent decline of a certain collective action frame.

It is widely acknowledged that any protest event is a symbolic action; and symbolism of the winter protest campaign of 2011-2012 in Russia was marked by many scholars. Regina Smyth, Anton Sobolev and Irina Sobolev have done useful research of symbolic effects of the pro-Putin rallies—a counter-campaign that was organised by the Kremlin in February-March of 2012 to confront the street actions of opposition.[9] To my mind, the analysis of symbolism of public representations of opposition attitudes could significantly contribute to understanding of the rise and failure of the street protest of 2011-2012. Doing it I focus on protest events that took place in Moscow, as far as, at first, they were a real driver of the whole campaign and have received more media coverage, and are also much better documented.

I start with discussion of theoretical issues concerning symbolic aspects of social protest in general and in the electoral authoritarian regimes in particular, paying special attention to the effects of mediatisation and visualisation. Then I go on to an analysis of public representations of opposition to the Putin regime in the Moscow protest campaign, focusing on symbolic means of construction of the identity of the protesters. To do so I draw attention to the public discussions about "modernisation," the "middle class" and "corruption" that, in my opinion, contributed to self-conception of the protest movement. Finally, I argue that a decline of the protest movement after June 2012 was facilitated by re-interpretation of its frames by its opponents that turned to be more plausible, on the one hand, because it relied upon better-established meanings, and on the other hand, because with Putin's re-election the context of symbolic contestation changed significantly.

Social Protest as Symbolic Politics and Its Effects for Electoral Authoritarian Regimes

Protest events, i.e., "challenges to authority embodied by collective actors in public settings,"[10] fulfil their function of contestation by making "visible" opposite attitudes, values and identities. In so doing, protesters challenge not only the particular policy of authorities, but also a dominant vision of social reality. According to Benford and Hunt, "social movements can be described as dramas in which protagonists and antagonists compete to affect audiences' interpretations of power relations in a variety of domains, including those pertaining to religious, political, economic, or lifestyle arrangements."[11] For this reason, the social protest could be analysed not only from the perspective of collective action theory, but also in terms of *symbolic politics*, i.e., activity aimed at articulation and promotion of competing visions of social reality.

The latter field of research is less elaborate and rather fragmented. The path-breaking works of Murray Edelman[12] did not induce a consistent research programme. However, there is an increasing set of literature focusing on production, articulation, dissemination and contestation of shared meanings as an inherent aspect of any political process.[13] Being oriented to the study of the whole range of forms in which meanings are articulated and contested, the symbolic policy approach perfectly fits into an analysis of the social movements counter-narratives as far as the latter quite often do not look like consistent ideologies, but rather take a form of diverse combination of verbalised ideas, symbolic actions and visual images that carry certain messages.

It should be mentioned that the researchers of social movement significantly contributed to this research field by elaborating useful analytical tools and making interesting empirical observations (usually without labelling it "symbolic politics"). Since the end of the 1980s they paid much attention to "the process through which individuals recognise that they share certain orientations in common and on that basis decide to act together,"[14] which they described in terms of collective identity and collective action frames. The latter concept was adopted from Irwin Goffman, however it was also widely used in psychiatry and cognitive psychology, referring to "an interpretative schemata that simplifies and condenses the 'world out there' by selectively punctuating and encoding objects, situations, events, experiences, and sequences of actions within one's present or past environment."[15] The concept of frame is more context-sensitive and agent-oriented than broader concepts like mentalities or political culture.[16] It allows one to focus on the process of production of meanings: collectively shared frames are results of framing as "an active phenomenon that implies agency and contention at the level of reality construction."[17] It also makes possible conceptual linking of collective and individual beliefs by analysis of frame alignment. As a result, the concept of collective action frame is a useful tool for analysis of symbolic dimension of the protest campaign. Scholars of the social movements also contributed to the latter approach trying to conceptualise collective actions as social performances (dramaturgical approach)[18] and as visual phenomena.[19]

Protest rallies are syncretic forms of public communication that include verbal, performative, action oriented and visual components. They have to compensate the relative inequality of access to traditional media by usage of expressive and suggestive means of articulation. Since the beginning of modern "mass politics" visual signs were essential means of identification of protesters and their claims.[20] Contemporary social movements use a broad range of visible expressions of dissent, like banners, flags, posters, symbolic signs, colours, gestures, etc. Protest actions are often deliberately staged as a performance based on various kinds of symbolism. So, analysis of visual representations of protest is definitely useful for study of public contestation of hegemonic systems of meanings that is an indispensable part of any social movement.

Production and distribution of dissent images and narratives depend on what Mattoni and Teune call "media-historical constellations," that is "available technical opportunities for producing and distributing images."[21] Proliferation of computer-mediated communication (mobile smartphones, social network sites, etc.) created a new context for social movements: production and distribution of protest images became possible without professional skills and expensive resources. It gave them new opportunities to bring their messages to the out-groups, and also to shape the collective memory of social movement and to construct its identity. This makes urgent the discussions about the relationship between the Internet and the growth of political protest in the world ("Twitter Revolution," etc.). However, in the contemporary media-historical constellation "traditional" media (in particular TV), that are easier to be controlled by the authorities, still play a major role. That is why the opportunities for distribution of messages of protest social movements depend not only on a "media-historical constellation," but also on the structure of the particular media-system.

Contestation of the dominant vision of social reality is an inherent part of protest movements that is peculiarly important for authoritarian regimes, many of which pay lip service to democracy and have elections. Such regimes are based not so much on coercion as on manipulation that creates a kind of "manageable consent." As Regina Smyth et al. put it, "In Electoral Authoritarian Regimes, projecting a regime-friendly political reality, one in which there is only one leader who can ensure national stability or in which an inviolable national unity is critical to maintaining regime support."[22] Stability of such regimes depends on maintenance of elite unity and on demonstration of its invincibility and impression of permanence.[23] Both characteristics are threatened by public protest: it weakens the authority of the rulers making "visible" the lack of consent. In the words of Graeme Robertson, "while it takes millions of voters to signal the weakness of a regime in elections, relatively small numbers of protesters in the streets, even in the low thousands, can raise questions about regime invincibility, leading others to join in."[24] That is why the Russian authorities take mass protest actions rather seriously and react with a broad range of means that includes not only direct coercion, but also symbolic counteraction and institutional changes. Some scholars suppose that the protest campaign of 2011-2012 has significantly transformed the political regime in Russia.[25] According to my argument developed elsewhere,[26] it undermined the hegemony of government discourse that before 2011 was deliberately syncretic and vague, and urged to design a more consistent state ideology to mobilise a "majority" against a "minority." So, in spite of the fact that protesters presented a small minority and actually did not propose a serious alternative programme, their contest had significant consequences for the political regime in Russia, and this happened not so much because of "real" threats but because of their perception, i.e., meanings ascribed to the events by the proponents, opponents, observers and bystanders.

In December 2011 the Russian authorities found themselves involved in a dynamic interaction with the protesting groups that had an essential symbolic dimension. In the next part of the article I am going to analyse public representations of the opposition to Putin's regime (including visual ones) in Moscow 2011-2012 protest campaign. As it would be difficult to analyse all relevant aspects this article will focus on framing the collective identity of the protesters, because to my mind the appearance at the public arena of a significant group challenging the regime was a crucial aspect of the "unexpected protest."

Collective identity is considered an important component of collective action frames that "refers to the process of defining this 'we,' typically in opposition to some 'they' who have different interests or values."[27] Following Alberto Melucci I understand *collective identity* as "a process in which actors produce the common cognitive frameworks that enable them to assess their environment and to calculate the costs and benefits of their action."[28]

It is a dynamic and reactive process that essentially relies on existing repertoires of symbols and meanings[29] and includes interaction between the opposing sides, as well as within each of the camp. The "resonance" of the frames articulated by protesters depends not only on their content (i.e., their consistency, cultural relevance and congruence to articulated claims), but also on "apparent fit between the framing and events in the world."[30] Hence, it is inevitably changeable and context-related. According to R. Benford and D. Snow, "hypothetically, the more culturally believable the claimed evidence, and the greater the number of slices of such evidence, the more credible the framing and the broader its appeal."[31] To my mind, this supposition gives a good clue for explanation of the dynamic of the 2011-2012 protest campaign.

Framing the Collective Identity of Protesters: The Analysis of Public Representations of Opposition to Putin's Regime

What further turned to become a protest campaign started with a spontaneous meeting in Moscow near Chistye Prudy metro station on December, 5, 2011, a day after the Russian Central Election Commission declared the results of the State Duma elections; the protesters claimed that the victory gained by the ruling United Russia Party (49 per cent of votes) was the result of a fraud. As the meeting was not officially permitted, some participants were detained. However, it did not stop the protesters, but gave an impetus for organisational efforts that resulted in a much larger meeting at Bolotnaya Square on December, 10, 2011 with about 50-60 thousand participants and to further the expansion of the protest movement in Moscow as well as in several large cities.[32] The Internet played a major role in the mobilisation of the protest movement and in shaping the public's views about the fairness of the election.[33] What was also significant, since the rally of December 10, protest activity has been covered by the central channels of Russian television (which typically did not happen with the protest before[34]).

However, it is clear that availability of means of dissemination of the protesters' messages was necessary but not a sufficient condition for their mobilisation. Their resonance has to do with diagnostic, prognostic and motivational framing[35] that appealed to some individuals and paved the way to construction of "we" against "them" identity. Of course, formation of social groups that could be sensitive to such framing should be considered a consequence of the relative economic prosperity of the 2000s, but their mobilisation was a result of a fusion of certain beliefs and meanings that were available in the cultural context. Three major public issues discussed in the previous years would be particularly important as sources of relevant ideas—that of "modernisation," the "middle class" and "corruption."

The concept of "modernisation" was coined as the official marker of President Dmitry Medvedev's political course in 2009. It evidently answered the need for change that in the context of the global economic crisis seemed unquestionable even for the conservatives, and was vague enough to allow a wide spectrum of different interpretations. Actually, Medvedev himself used the term in more than one sense, and probably did it not without purpose; in his rhetoric "modernisation" referred to particular economic tasks as well as to future changes of the Russian society including supposed (but never clearly articulated) political reforms.[36] So, public discussions about "modernisation" took the form of competition of different programmes, or rather aspirations for future development of Russia. Loaded with numerous meanings, the term "modernisation" supported expectations for some changes even if it was often perceived as a pure ideological tool. It was associated with Medvedev[37] who was considered a more liberal "partner" in the "power tandem" that took place in 2008-2012 (with former president Vladimir Putin as Prime Minister).

The issue of the "middle class" eventually became associated with discussions about "modernisation," though actually it was put into public agenda earlier. In 2007 Putin included this topic in his Annual Address to the Federal Assembly, and in 2008 when discussing the strategy of development of Russia till 2020 he announced the task of raising the part of the "middle class" to 60 or even 70 per cent of the total population. This opened a way for intensive expert discussions that were willingly covered by the media. Under closer consideration (and after certain manipulation with criteria) the size of the "middle class" turned to be larger than was previously expected. In the autumn of 2008, in the context of economic crisis the "middle class" was routinely mentioned as an actually existing group that falls under risk and should be rescued. And in 2009 it was declared the main beneficiary and driver of "modernisation." What was important, in all public discussions about the "middle class" was its representation as a bearer of social characteristics that were considered important for economic and political development: it was portrayed as a group that is "disposed to innovations," "self-reliant and emancipate from the state," "is interested in democratisation of politics," "self-respectful," etc.[38] As we shall see, this repertoire of meanings was actively used for framing self-representations of protesters. The concept of the "middle class" was not entirely new for the Russian public discourse, however previously it was not used to describe an already existing social group. So, in some sense it proposed a new frame of identification whose plausibility depended on personal experience. It could be assumed that it seemed more relevant to those who could use it as self-description (as it was positive); while the others could be more disposed for better established binary categories, like "wealthy" vs. "poor," "the Muscovites" vs. "the provincials" or "the intelligentsia" vs. "the ordinary people."

In contrast to the first two topics, the issue of "corruption" was brought to the public agenda against the will of the authorities. This discussion was initiated by civic activists; the major role in it was played by blogger Alexey Naval'ny who systematically published material about corruption of the state officials paying special attention to the ruling United Russia Party. The meme "PZhIV" invented by Naval'ny—an acronym for "The Party of Crooks and Thieves" (*Partijazhulikov i vorov*)—became one of the key slogans of counter-campaign of the opposition during elections to the State Duma and was later used to frame the identity of opponents of the protest movement.

Protests were triggered by the announcement in September 2011 about Putin's decision to run in the forthcoming presidential election. For a long time the partners of the "tandem" were intrigued about the nominee for the next presidential term. Putin's decision was not unexpected. However the way it was performed—Putin and Medvedev declared their "castling" (as it was labelled by press) at the Congress of the United Russia Party without real discussion—cynically demonstrated the political insignificance of the formally ruling party as well as of the will of the electorate.[39] This scenario of power transmission was reminiscent of the Soviet era and symbolised the end of expectations of changes inspired by the rhetoric of "modernisation." Even if such expectations were rather hesitant, the perception of their failure after the "castling" was quite certain. Such demonstrative disdain of the people's will could not but arouse an emotional protest. Added with criticism of corruption and general dissatisfaction with government's policy in the context of the crisis, it stimulated a significant decline of support of the United Russia before the State Duma election (according to surveys of WCIOM—the most "pro-Kremlin" pollster organisation—its electoral rating had decreased from 43 per cent in September to 35 per cent on the eve of the December elections[40]). Relying on these figures, its capacity to get the overwhelming majority as it used to do before was problematic. However, there was a common belief that the results of the elections would be rigged. It stimulated many civic organisations and independent individuals to take the status of observers at the State Duma elections; as a result, after the election day (December 4, 2011) the Internet was inflated with video material and witness accounts documenting the facts of fraud.

The behaviour of the observers and those who were inspired by their information and came to the rally "For Fair Elections" disclaimed the identity of passive "electorate" supposed by Putin's scenario of power transmission. It created a new framework of political identity that did not coincide with that of "the old" opposition that was either integrated into the system of "the managed democracy" or marginalised as the Yabloko Party. The "new" opposition was framed in terms of "the civic society" rather than party politics. The claim for "fair elections" united different political forces, like the Liberals and the Russian nationalists, but also many individuals who did not belong to any political organisation. According to Samuel Greene, the "newness" of the protest movement of 2011-2012 had to do with "the creation of new ties and relationships among already existing protest groups, which in turn allowed them to present a mobilisation argument that proved much more powerful than anything that had previously been on the table."[41] This mobilisation argument was developed not so much in the formal programmes (under the given circumstances, the points of consensus could not be broad and emotionally appealing), but in the frames of collective action that were articulated by the newly arrived leaders of the protest movement, as well as by its participants and observers. Constructing the collective identity of the newly emerging group of dissenters was the central component of this framing process as the very fact of its existence challenged the illusion of national unity and invincibility of the regime. Besides, in spite of frames of injustice and agency[42] this aspect has not got enough attention in literature.

The framing took place in official documents of the protest movement, statements of its leaders, publications of traditional media and online discussions in the social networks, but also in the numerous visual representations at the protest rallies. The latter source is particularly interesting for understanding a symbolic dimension of the protest. According to the authors of the collective volume *My ne nemy (We are not Dumb)* published in Tartu, a mass usage of the self-made "requisite"—posters, badges, flags, carnival suites, etc.—was a feature of the 2011-2012 campaign in comparison with the previous protest actions. They relate it to the fact that many participants did not belong to any organisations and to their social profiles: "a significant part of the participants were brilliant and creative people who did not want to be a part of a faceless crowd," and self-made posters were "means of individual self-expression."[43] All these were pictured and disseminated on the Internet, collected by field researches, but also reposted and commented on in social networks. They worked as a good tool for communicating frames of a rather decentralised and heterogeneous protest movement.

The analysis of these and other material reveals clear attempts to construct the identity of the protesters as a group. This intention is well symbolised by the slogan *Vynasdazhe ne predstavliaete (You don't even represent—but also, don't know—us)* presented at the meeting in St. Petersburg on December 10 and actively reposted on the Internet.[44] It was very important to demonstrate that protesters are *not a small* minority. Official reports systematically underestimated the size of the protest rallies, and inflated numbers of the pro-regime ones. And here visual evidence—pictures of the crowds occupying vast spaces at Bolotnaya Square (December, 10) and Sakharov Avenue (December 24)—gave visual evidence of the significance of the protesting group.

The same purpose was achieved by visualisation of belonging with the White Ribbon that became a symbol of the protest campaign. Conventional signs are often used for identification of protesters and their sympathisers; wearing ribbons of particular colour, flowers or badges—and not only during public action, but also before and after it—is an easy way to demonstrate solidarity with a social movement and at the same time to visualise its presence in the society. It seems the White Ribbon was a ready-made idea: this symbol had been already used in a similar context (it had more than one origin); the website for its propagation was created a few weeks before the mass protest actions. It facilitated quick dissemination of the symbol. Its symbolic potential was even raised by quick reaction of the main opponent: on December 15, 2011 Vladimir Putin tried to denigrate the White Ribbon during his "direct line"—mega-interview to the central TV channels—when he first identified the signs on the clothes of protesters as "contraceptives." It was hardly a good idea as Putin's words gave an occasion for numerous jokes with sexual implications (like posters with Putin's portrait and texts: *Eto ne nashprezik* (affectionate dinimutive from: "This is not our president (but also 'condom')" or *Nam ne nuzhenispol'zovannyj president!!* ("We do not need a used-up president!").[45] However, later, when the counterstrategy of the authorities became firmer and the idea of support to the protest campaign from abroad came to be central, the symbolism of the White Ribbon was used against the protesters: it was associated with the white flag of capitulation before the enemy, for example, demotivators with the text: *Nadel Beluju Lentu—kapitulirovalpered NATO* ("If you put on a White Ribbon, you have capitulated before the NATO"). So, from the very beginning the White Ribbon became a matter of contestation.

The campaign "for fair elections" was not only a struggle for nullification of the results of unfair elections and organisation of new ones (which probably was not realistic). It was also a public demonstration of particular attitudes that challenged Putin's scenario of power transmission and some "constitutive principles of Russian state power."[46] It represented the existence of an ever-growing group of citizens who demanded recognition of their rights and protested against falsification of their votes. This group claimed to be "the people" whose will should be respected (as it was written at self-made posters demonstrated on Sakharov Avenue on December 24: "People, you are democracy, you are changes, you are the future!", "We woke up, this is only a beginning!"). Visual materials demonstrated by rallies' participants came into dialogue with discourse of Putin, Medvedev and other state officials pointing to their incompetence and misunderstanding of the reality. Protesters invented witty responses to attempts of their opponents to downplay their collective identity. Answering to Putin's jokes about "contraceptives," to his comparison of the protesters with "the Bandar-logs"—garrulous and fussy monkeys from the animated cartoon "Mowgli" (from Rudyard Kipling's "The Jungle Book"[47]) or to his insinuations about being paid by the US State Department, the authors of the posters represented themselves as responsible, self-sufficient and self-respecting citizens with a good sense of humour who are capable of demanding responsibility from state officials.

The expansion of the protest movement in the first weeks after the Duma elections evidently confirmed an embarrassment and relative weakness of the authorities. Attempts of the state officials to reply to the claims of the protesters, even if they were intended to depreciate their identity, meant their recognition as a group. The "unexpected protest" became a matter of intensive public communications which also raised issues about the "visualisation" of the new identity. In the media it was labelled the "middle" or the "creative" class, which facilitated employment of the positive frames shaped in the discussions about "modernisation" and the "middle" class.

However, as all symbolic constructions, the frames of collective identity of the protesters were open for reinterpretation. And the pro-Kremlin propagandists had done their best to denigrate it. The protesters were represented as a *minority* that went against the pro-Putin *majority* thus pretending to a status that overwhelms its real democratic "weight." They were described in terms of well-established binary oppositions: as prospering and satiated inhabitants of the capital cities vs. hard-working and indigent provincials, as "intelligentsia" vs. "working people," as "not authentic" representatives of the nation vs. "the real" people. The very opportunity of raising the "middle class" who was considered a kernel of "the angry city dwellers" *(rasserzhennyegorozhane)* was claimed to be a result of Putin's policy. Finally, the protesters were accused of being connected with the foreign (in particular, the American) secret services which made them tools of the enemies of Russia. These reinterpretations were made even more salient by organisation since February 2012 pro-Putin rallies that not only confirmed the support of the leading candidate for presidency, but also articulated the opposing identity of the "patriotic majority" using approximately the same set of symbolic instruments.

Conclusion

Finally, the counter-representation of the protesting groups as non-patriotic, alien to "the ordinary people," conceited and ungrateful "anti-national" minority turned to be successful. Alongside with toughening the legal regulation of public demonstrations, direct coercion against individual oppositionists and huge inequality of resources, it was a major factor of the decline of protest movement after June 2012. Pro-regime propagandists had reinterpreted the frames of self-representation used by protesters, loading them with negative meaning, and created alternative frames of interpretation that evidently resonated to a "new Putin's majority" (which definitely was facilitated but not predetermined by unequal access to media channels). The collective identity of "the exigent citizens" claiming for "fair elections" that seemed convincing in the context of "weakening" of the power in the period of the presidential election, has lost its plausibility after Putin's inauguration and strengthening of the regime. With political turmoil being over, the case of the opposition who finally was not able to propose a realistic alternative to the official course came to be rather problematic. It facilitated a negative inversion of the sets of beliefs and meanings that served for self-representation of the protesters: an image of self-reliant, educated and successful "middle class" citizens claiming a corrupted government for accountability gave a way to that of well-to-do and problem-free inhabitants of the capital-cities who were inspired by foreign ideas (if not paid by foreign money) and could not share actual concerns of the "ordinary Russian people." While the former image developed relatively new frames shaped in the recent years, the latter relied on well-established meanings that described "the old" social cleavages. It made it convincing for many Russians thus contributing to marginalisation of the failed protesters.

Notes

1. See Julia Baskakova, "Otnedovol'stva k protestu: u porogasmenysostoianii" ("From Dissatisfaction to Protest: at the Threshold of Status Change") (in Rus.), in Sergey Patrushev (ed.), *Grazhdanskoe i politicheskoe v rossiiskikhobschestvennykhpraktikakh* (The Civic and the Political in the Russian public practices) (in Rus.), Moscow: ROSSPEN, 2013, pp. 354-77.
2. This infrastructure includes not only the means of suppression, but also a system of institutions that should integrate civil society groups into the state and isolate more adversarial groups and organisations. According to Graeme Robertson, these "inventions" "put the Putin administration at the cutting edge in the design of a contemporary postmodern authoritarianism that is increasingly common in the post-Cold War world." Graeme B. Robertson, "Managing Society: Protest, Civil Society, and Regime in Putin's Russia," *Slavic Review*, 68, no. 3, 2009, p. 532; cf. Robert Hovarth, "Putin's 'Preventive Counter-Revolution': Post-Soviet Authoritarianism and the Spectre of Velvet Revolution," *Europe-Asia Studies*, 63, no. 1, 201, pp. 1-25; Ilya Budraitskis, "The Weakest Link of Managed Democracy: How the Parliament Gave Birth to Non-Parliamentary Politics," *The South Atlantic Quarterly*, 113, no. 1, 2014, pp. 169-85.
3. Veronika Shishkina, "Politicheskii protest v dinamikeprotestnykhnastroenii (Political Protest in the Dynamics of Protest Attitudes), in *Grazhdanskoe i politicheskoe v rossiiskikhobschestvennykhpraktikakh*, p. 382.
4. Mikhail Dmitriev, "Lost in Transition? The Geography of Protests and Attitude Change in Russia," *Europe-Asia Studies*, 67, no. 2, 2015, p. 224. Some scholars prefer the term "the creative class" (Irina Busygina and Mikhail Filippov, "The Calculus of Non-Protest in Russia: Redistributive Expectations from Political Reforms," *Europe-Asia Studies*, 67, no. 2, 2015, pp. 219-20).

5. As I shall demonstrate below, the "middle class" hypothesis was actively exploited in mass media. Practically all scholars who explore it do it with some reservations.
6. See Evgeny Gontmakher and Cameron Ross, "The Middle Class and Democratisation in Russia," *Europe-Asia Studies*, 67, no. 2, 2015, pp. 281.
7. Dmitry Gromov, "Ulichnyipoliticheskiiaktcionismpozavchera i vchera" ("The Street Political Actionism the Day Before Yesterday and Yesterday") (in Rus.), in *"My ne nemy": Antropologiaprotesta v Rossii 2011-2012 godov ("We are not Dumb": The Anthropology of the Protest in Russia, 2011-2012)*, compiled by Alexandra Arkhipova and Mikhail Alekseevskij, Tartu: ELM, 2014, p. 50.
8. Richard Sakwa, "Questioning Control and Contestation in Late Putinite Russia," *Europe-Asia Studies*, 67, no. 2, 2015, p. 192; cf. Ilya Budraitskis, "The Weakest Link of Managed Democracy: How the Parliament Gave Birth to Non-Parliamentary Politics."
9. Regina Smyth, Anton Sobolev, and Irina Soboleva, "A Well-Organised Play: Symbolic Politics and the Effect of the Pro-Putin Rallies," *Problems of Post-Communism*, 60, no. 2, 2013, pp. 24-39.
10. Thomas N. Ratliff and Lori L. Hall, "Practising the Art of Dissent: Toward a Typology of Protest Activity in the United States," *Humanity & Society*, 38, no. 3, 2014, p. 274.
11. Robert Benford and Scott A. Hunt. "Dramaturgy and Social Movements: The Social Construction and Communication of Power," *Sociological Inquiry*, 62, no. 1, 1992, p. 38.
12. Murrey Edelman, *The Symbolic Uses of Politics*, 5th ed., Urbana etc. (University of Illinois Press: 1972). Originally published in 1964; Murrey Edelman, *Politics as Symbolic Action. Mass Arousal and Quiescence* (Chicago: Markham Publishing Company, 1971).
13. For an overview, see Alison Brysk, "'Hearts and Minds': Bringing Symbolic Politics Back In," *Polity*, 27, no. 4, 1995, pp. 559-85.
14. Alberto Melucci, "Nomads of the Present: Social Movements and Individual Needs" in *Contemporary Society*, ed. by John Keane and Paul Mier (London: Hutchinson Radius, 1989), p. 30.
15. David A. Snow and Robert D. Benford, "Master Frames and Cycles of Protest," in Aldon D. Morris and Carol McClurg Mueller (eds.), *Frontiers in Social Movement Theory* (New Haven, etc.: Yale University Press, 1992), p. 137.
16. Sidney Tarrow, "Mentalities, Political Cultures, and Collective Action Frames: Constructing Meaning Through Action," in Morris and McClurg Mueller (eds.), *Frontiers in Social Movement Theory*, pp. 174-202.
17. Robert D. Benford and David A. Snow, "Framing Process and Social Movements: An Overview and Assessment," *Annual Review of Sociology*, 26, 2000, p. 613. According to the definition of R. Benford and D. Snow, "collective action frames are action-oriented sets of beliefs and meanings that inspire and legitimate the activists and campaigns of a social movement organisation," p. 614.
18. Robert Benford and Scott A. Hunt, ibid.; Ron Eyerman, "Performing Opposition Or, How Social Movements Move," in Jeffrey C. Alexander, Bernard Giesen and Jason L. Mast (eds.), *Social Performance: Symbolic Action, Cultural Pragmatics, and Ritual* (Cambridge: Cambridge University Press, 2006), pp. 193-217.
19. Thomas N. Ratliff and Lori L. Hall, "Practising the Art of Dissent," Tim F. Liao, "Visual Symbolism, Collective Memory, and Social Protest: A Study of the 2009 London G20 Protest," *Social Alternatives*, 29, no. 3, 2010, pp. 37-43; Alice Mattoni and Simon Teune, "Visions of protests. A media-historic perspective on images in social movements," *Sociology Compass*, 8, no. 6, 2014, pp. 876-87.

20. See for example Eric Hobsbawm, "Mass-Producing Traditions: Europe, 1870-1914," in Eric Hobsbawm and Terence Ranger (eds.), *The Invention of Tradition* (Cambridge, etc.: Cambridge University Press, 1983), pp. 283-86.
21. Alice Mattoni and Simon Teune, "Visions of protests."
22. Regina Smyth, Anton Sobolev and Irina Soboleva, "A Well-Organised Play," p. 26.
23. Graeme B. Robertson, "Managing Society...," pp. 531-32.
24. Robertson, "Managing Society...," p. 531.
25. Richard Sakwa, "Questioning Control and Contestation in Late Putinite Russia," pp. 203-5; Ilya Budraitskis, "The Weakest Link of Managed Democracy."
26. Olga Malinova, "'Spiritual Bonds' as State Ideology: Opportunities and Limitations," *Russia in Global Affairs*, no. 4, 2014, http://eng.globalaffairs.ru/number/Spiritual-Bonds-as-State-Ideology-17223 (accessed June 8, 2015).
27. William A. Gamson, *Talking Politics* (Cambridge, etc.: Cambridge University Press, 1992), p. 7. Gamson also distinguishes between the injustice component and the agency component.
28. Alberto Melucci, *Nomads of the Present,* p. 35.
29. Sidney Tarrow, "Mentalities, Political Cultures, and Collective Action Frames," p. 189.
30. Robert D. Benford and David A. Snow, "Framing Process and Social Movements," pp. 619-21.
31. Ibid., 620.
32. For a description of chronology of the campaign, see Samuel A. Greene, "Beyond Bolotnaia. Bridging Old and New in Russia's Election Protest Movement," *Problems of Post-Communism*, 60, no. 2, 2013, pp. 41-42.
33. See Greene, "Beyond Bolotnaia," Stephen White and Ian McAllister, "Did Russia (Nearly) have a Facebook Revolution in 2011? Social Media's Challenge to Authoritarianism," *Politics*, 34, no. 1 , 2014, pp. 72–84; Regina Smyth and Sarah Oates, "Mind the Gaps: Media Use and Mass Action in Russia," *Europe-Asia Studies*, 67, no. 2, 2015, pp. 285-305.
34. Cf. Dennis Zuev, "A Visual Dimension of Protest: An Analysis of Interactions during the Russian March," *Visual Anthropology*, 23, 2010, p. 222.
35. See Robert D. Benford and David A. Snow, "Framing Process and Social Movements," pp. 615-17.
36. See Olga Malinova, "Eschoodinryvok? Obrazykollektivnogoproshlogo, nastoiaschego i buduschego v sovremennykhdiskussijakh o modernizatsii" ("One more spurt? Representations of the national past, present and future in the contemporary discussions about modernization"), *Politicheskaianauka*, no. 2, 2012, pp. 49-72.
37. It turned to be correct, as soon after his re-election in 2012 Vladimir Putin eliminated the term "modernisation" from his rhetoric.
38. See Olga Malinova and Valentina Efremova, "Politicheskieeksperty i 'srednijklass': analizpublichnykhdiskussij" ("Political experts and the 'middle class': An analysis of the public discussions,") (in Rus.), in Olga Malinova (ed.), *Simvolicheskaiapolitika: Spory o proshlomkakproektirovaniebuduschego* (*Symbolic politics: Discussions about the past as Projections of the Future* (in Rus.) (Moscow: INION RAS, 2014), pp. 326-43.
39. Cf. Regina Smith, "The Putin Factor: Personalism, Protest, and Regime Stability in Russia," *Politics & Policy*, 42, no. 4, 2014, p. 569.
40. WCIOM. Press-vypusk no. 1910, http://wciom.ru/index.php?id=236&uid=112199
41. Samuel A. Greene, "Beyond Bolotnaia," p. 41.

42. See Daria Radchenko, Dina Pisarevskaia and Irina Ksenofontova, "Logikavirtual'nogoprotesta: Internet poslevyborov" ("Logic of the Virtual Protest: Internet after the Elections"), in *"My ne nemy": Antropologiaprotesta v Rossii 2011-2012 godov*: 19-44; Samuel A. Greene, "Beyond Bolotnaia"; Ilya Budraitskis, "The Weakest Link of Managed Democracy," p. 183.
43. Mikhail Alekseevskij, "Ktovseetiljudi (s plakatami)?" ("Who are all those people (with posters)?" (in Rus.), in *"My ne nemy": Antropologiaprotesta v Rossii 2011-2012 godov*, p. 79.
44. *"My ne nemy": Antropologiaprotesta v Rossii 2011-2012,* p. 64.
45. *"My ne nemy," p.* 212.
46. Anton N. Oleinik, "Mass Protests in the Context of the Russian Power Regime," *Russian Social Science Review*, 54, no. 3, 2013, p. 95.
47. For analysis of visual "replies" to Putin's depreciating phrases, see Maria Akhmetova, "Vokrugbanderlogov," in: *"My ne nemy": Antropologiaprotesta v Rossii 2011-2012 godov*, pp. 165-96.

5. The Politics of Exclusion: Rhetoric, Symbolism and Gezi Park

Anita Sengupta

Rhetoric remains one of the most interesting and debated aspect of political communication and in its turn the rhetoric that particular events generate becomes an important part of the political process. Since politics is a continual struggle over meanings and signification, understanding the political process requires an analysis of how the symbolic enters the political process, how political actors consciously or unconsciously manipulate symbols through rhetoric and how this relates to the material bases of power. Literature that explores political symbolism now propose that alongside analysis that centres on power and interests, consideration of political symbolism and rhetoric provides useful insights that evoke political recognition, promoting normative or positive ideas about politics.[1] Political action of all types involves meanings for participants and observers irrespective of long term consequences or effects. The increased media exposure of those who exercise political power means that symbols, gestures, rhetoric and gimmicks are now symbolically constituted and examined.

Studies of political symbolism have traditionally argued that much of the mechanics of modern liberal democracy can be understood in terms of meanings it generates for the polity as much as the functions it fulfils.[2] As such, the ritualistic aspects of voting are as important as the vote that is cast. While certain political actions, emblems and signs invoke meanings that can be delineated from a literal understanding of the signs involved, certain other actions and images, produce meanings that are both widely understood and evoke defined responses.[3] Symbols, however, are not always uncontested and the ability of symbols to invoke different meanings or their *multi-vocality* has been the subject of analysis.[4] Often there is contestation between those who evoke the symbols and those who are subject to them. In fact, at times, power has been derived from the control over a society's symbols.[5]

Rhetoric and symbolism are interwoven and convenient ways to reach the target as they are routinely relayed by the press. The power of rhetoric resides principally in the power of metaphor. But rhetoric is also sometimes a term of abuse and can be made to refer to disagreement. Along with symbolism and myths, rhetoric performs a key role in political communication and propaganda. While in most situations rhetoric is invoked for inclusion, in some it performs the role of exclusion. This became evident during the incidents following the Gezi Park protests when a sharp differentiation was recognised, in the political rhetoric of the leadership among followers of the AKP (*Adalet ve Kalkinma Partisi* or Justice and Development Party) and those who had opposed its policies in the course of the protests. The events started when a small environmentalist group protested against the neoliberal "urban renewal" plan by the AKP and the then Prime Minister Recep Tayyip Erdogan, in order to protect Gezi Park, one of the rare green areas in the Taksim area of Istanbul. In a purely symbolic act the protests started exactly a month after the suppression of the First of May demonstrations and took unprecedented proportions by converting itself into a massive social movement. While most activists have subsequently talked about planning for a social movement that had been in place for some time, there is also a general agreement that Gezi provided a spontaneous and unexpected trigger.

In an article called "The Gezi Resistance as Surplus Value"[6] the author argues that the surplus value that Gezi generated was in terms of meanings, praxis and "publicness" that it generated. The symbolism that Gezi Park produced was something that the political leadership found difficult to comprehend, and the contradiction between qualifying the protests as "concern for a few trees" and simultaneously an "international plot" was reflective of this. The government, however, was not alone in the race to appropriate the symbolic value of the protests. Gezi Park also generated rhetoric from among the protesters who contributed their own subversive slogans and visual images. The Gezi Park protesters were exceedingly good at developing a discourse by using a strong sense of humour, incorporating music into their power of opposition and employing the social media. This article is an attempt to examine both the rhetoric of exclusion generated by the ruling establishment and the counter-rhetoric generated by the protesters who in a number of cases inverted the same rhetoric to their advantage.

The Site of the Protest

Gezi Park, which was the original locus of demonstrations that spread across Turkey, has long served as the spatial centre of political struggles. Once standing in its stead were the Ottoman artillery barracks, built in the early 1800s, which were the initial manifestation of a long process of Ottoman modernisation. The barracks then became the site of the counterrevolution of 1909 that developed vis-à-vis the Young Turks who toppled the regime of the Ottoman Sultan Abdulhamid II a year earlier. The barracks were demolished in 1940 under the Turkish Republican regime and replaced by Gezi Park as part of the broader vision for the development of Taksim Square. The complexity of this history of urban space reflects the political culture it has come to signify. Turkish modernisation remains an attempt to introduce as many modern elements as the national elite deemed necessary and useful. The Turkish nation had to be modern, but at the same time obedient to the national elites. As a result only the national elite defined the public space and the rules by which politics should be conducted. Thus, a monolithic national ideology was shaped, while at the same time social diversity was used as an obstacle to the development of a civil society and as a hindrance to questioning the terms under which the political community was structured. The Gezi protest was the first in recent Turkish history to have presented the claim for democracy in Turkey, a claim made in the name of inclusive politics and against the dualism of Kemalism–Islamism.

Events unfolded when a call went out on May 28 for people to defend the Taksim Gezi Park against bulldozers that had appeared overnight to uproot trees as a first step towards replacing the park with a reconstruction of the historic Taksim Military Barracks demolished in 1940. The initial alert came from Taksim Solidarity, an umbrella platform that had been organised to spearhead movements against urban transformation projects that characterise the AKP's urban policy. This includes environmentally destructive infrastructural projects like the third Bosporus Bridge and the Istanbul Canal and the privatisation of formerly public spaces like the Gezi Park. What began with a small group of people keeping watch over the trees rapidly grew into round-the-clock occupation of the park with the number of people increasing every day. When police used tear-gas and water cannons on the occupants and set up barricades to keep them out, there was a wave of protest that has continued ever since and has been replicated in sixty-seven cities from Ankara to Ismir, Adana and Hatay.

The make-up and content of the protests have varied widely from city to city with different slogans and symbols. The millions of people who have joined in the movement were, however, united by two broad concerns: a sense of frustration with Erdogan and his party's approach to governance on a range of issues, and anger at the violent response of the police and failure of mainstream Turkish media to cover it. It was the brutal repression and violent behaviour of the state authorities that triggered the massive support to the initial protesters and turned the protest into Turkey's biggest anti-government movement in decades. Gezi also turned a once-popular leader into a sultan—or a "democratic dictator" who considered suppression as the only possible way to silence millions of opposition voices.

In the span of a few days, Erdogan made a number of negative statements, particularly against non-AKP voters. In the process he also managed to bring together many diverse groups (from Kemalists to leftists to environmentalists to LGBT to Kurds, even Islamists who had supported the AKP but no longer agreed with its policies) in opposition to authoritarianism and state paternalism, as well as to struggle for unity in diversity. This coalition of diverse groups and the fight for the public space and democratic participation created a new dynamic that demanded to be heard, not only in elections, but at all times and to have a say in governance. What is also significant is that the movement was led by neither the Left nor other political groups. It was a movement whose energy and dynamics was derived from people belonging to different groups, but who all had something in common, the anti-authoritarian spirit that acts as an element of resistance to anything that is linked with authoritarian state authority. This enhanced political engagement initially resulted from environmental consciousness and was subsequently converted into opposition towards Erdogan's pejorative statements on secular lifestyles along with the necessity of standing up against the pressure of majoritarianism that rules out civil liberties for minority groups.

The Politics of Exclusion

While struggle for control over the public space of the Gezi Park became a matter of controversy, Erdogan's rhetoric was polarising. In fact a neologism *Chapulling* was introduced in Turkish political lexicon when Erdogan referred to the demonstrators at the Gezi Park and elsewhere as *capulcu*:

> We cannot watch some capulcu inciting our people …. Yes we will also build a mosque. I do not need permission for this; neither from the head of the Republican People's Party (CHP) nor from a few capulcu. I got permission from the fifty per cent of the citizens who elected us as the governing party.[7]

The term was quickly appropriated by the demonstrators to mean fighting for your rights. In June 2013 the Turkish Patent Institute received 16 applications for capulcu related trademarks, covering items such as drinks and newspapers.

On a far more serious note Gezi Park and the subsequent protests led to new definitions of the "margin" within Turkey with state recognition of a sharp differentiation between supporters of the AKP and those who opposed its policies in the course of the protests throughout Turkey. Erdogan claimed to govern 50% of the population who have repeatedly voted for the party thereby marginalising the rest who have been frustrated about the government's stand on issues ranging from property development and media rights to the role of religion and access to alcohol, all of which is viewed as attempts to impose conservative values on a secular society. Being "marginal" thereby acquired the political overtones that define belonging in terms of ideological convergence.

Post-Gezi Park the self-definition of the marginal in Turkey also changed and I cite from a piece called "In support of the Margin."

> All the groups labelled as "marginal" by the city governor and the prime minister is legal. Most of these groups are in fact leftists and revolutionary organisations. And precisely because they routinely come under attack by the state, harassed in their assemblies and protests, taken under detention without charges and choked in gas despite being legal and legitimate social organisations, they know state violence well and know even better how to resist it. Those groups labelled as "marginal" have always carried their flags and banners through which they claimed their existence in the squares of Turkey. For example, the Kurdish "Yurtsever" youth have always carried and still carry the banners of Abdullah Ocalan, their choice of a leader, demanding his liberation. Another example is the anarchists who carry a black flag and struggle for a society without the imposition of a state … Although they all operate on legal grounds and subsequently partake in

> the formation named as the "Taksim Solidarity Platform" they have been continuously, systematically, and in every space imaginable, rendered as convicts of a grey place. Because they struggle in this grey space in social life, whereby the line between legality and illegality is being blurred by state violence itself, the conventional adjective that comes to mind to label them in Turkey is indeed no other than "marginal."[8]

Nazan Ustundag goes on to point out that Gezi Park has become a revolt against marginalisation. He argues that the fifty per cent vote that the AKP administration received in the last two elections has advanced into a new phase, the one hundred-year-old "marginalise the ones who do not resemble you" in Turkey. Therefore, precisely because the AKP has aimed at marginalising each and every one of the fifty per cent of Turkey that did not resemble its constituents, that they have revolted against it on grounds of the Gezi Park. The state responded with the claim that it was "marginal groups" who occupied Gezi Park. The groups identified as marginal in Istanbul and elsewhere mainly hailed from the secular and liberal middle class. However, religious conservatives, the AKP's main voter base, have been equally uneasy with the events and with state responses. It was argued that Erdogan also stood to lose ground among the more secular conservatives. Faced with an outpouring of criticism against the government imposed restrictions on the consumption of alcohol, Erdogan told them to "go and drink at home" suggesting that there is no place in the public space for those who have preferences other than those prescribed by the government.

The protests involved the participation of people from every ideological position in Turkish politics, except for the supporters of the AKP themselves. The majority were middle-class and secular, but the participation of working-class people, practising Muslims and ethnic and religious minorities belied any attempt to characterise this movement as "being organised by extremist elements" and lacking public support as claimed by Erdogan. The positions and goals of the people participating in the demonstrations were diverse and sometimes incompatible but the common spirit of resistance was undeniable. The significance of the movement to "take back" the public space, the alignment of dissent and the slogans built around the threatened trees were extensively debated in the social media.

Most people who commented on the character of the movement stressed the fact that the movement was heterogeneous. It has also been stressed that the groups who gathered in Taksim and elsewhere were pressing for different demands. Many were protesting against Erdogan's style of governance, others found Turkey's staunch Kemalist identity to have diminished, there were environmentalist groups seeking protection of plants and trees against urbanisation, also included were groups aiming to get more labour rights from the country's expanding Holding Companies and Corporations.

Erdogan, however, argued that the unrest was not reflective of the legitimate grievances of the Turks:

> The protests were nothing more than the minority's attempt to dominate the majority .... We could not have allowed this and we will not allow it ...[9]

However, the events did not mark a turning point in domestic politics. Noteworthy as the demonstrators were for their resilience, Erdogan had a point when he said, "I would gather 200,000 where they gather 20 and where they gather 100,000, I would gather 1 million party supporters."[10] When it comes to sheer numbers, the government still enjoys a majority. The March 2014 local elections in fact gave the AKP around 45% of the votes, up from the 39% that the AKP received in the last local elections in 2009, indicating a huge victory for Erdogan. This has been interpreted to mean that Erdogan's policies and response to the popular unrest has not had an impact on the voting pattern, and a number of reasons have been cited for this.[11] Experts therefore noted that comparison of the Gezi Park protests with the Arab Spring was wrong as Erdogan was a democratically elected leader. However, they also argued that Erdogan's understanding of democracy seemed to be restricted to the ballot box.

> He thinks that by getting 50% of the votes in the last election, he can act as he wants to. But there are still 50% who did not elect him. This section of the Turkish society demands to be heard.[12]

The protests, though, have deeper implications which cannot be washed away by crude headcounts. The Turkish government is currently enmeshed in a double gamble, securing peace with the Kurds, seeing through the new civilian constitution but also dealing with the waves of Syrian refugees who now reside in Turkey and are being encouraged by the EU to remain there.

These are drawn out processes that will require engagement with all elements of Turkish society. This celebration of the majority has been matched by those who have indicated clearly that "democracy is not just what the majority wants. It is also about what the minority wants. Democracy is not just about elections."[13]

During the protests state officials used familial discourse as a way to define the parameters of the public sphere. The Mayor of Istanbul said that he has serious concerns about the safety of "our kids." This was repeated by Erdogan who warned parents to get their children under control. The protesters did not remain passive addressees of this political discourse. They engaged in the debate by subverting the political role assigned to the family by politicians:

> We are a belittled and mocked generation notorious for being apolitical. We are a generation ninety per cent of whom have never taken part in an ideological struggle and thought of street protests as futile and unnecessary obstacles ...[14]

Women of different generations and walks of life also participated in the movement.[15] While the image of the "lady in red" became symbolic of the excesses of the state, the alternative image that was proposed by the state was that of a young mother wearing a hijab who was harassed by the protesters. She was identified as the real representative of the protests rather than "the lady in red." However, even among them there were different reasons for protesting. A substantial number of them overlap with resistance to government interfacing with the female body. A significant role was also played by the paternalistic jargon that was generated by the leadership. Only a few identified themselves as feminists but the popular uprising constitutes a process of resistance whose language, form and ethics are produced on the streets. This was demonstrated by the arrival in Gezi Park of mothers whose children may or may not have been there on the eve of June 13. Responding to a call from the Mayor of Istanbul to "come and get your children" they formed a protective human chain around the protesters. This was also a protest against the government's political discourse whereby women are recognised in, and defined through, the domestic sphere. New kinds of solidarity were produced. Gezi Park brought them together with another group of mothers, *The Saturday Mothers,* who gathered to seek justice for unresolved cases involving state violence against political or Kurdish activists.

Erdogan's rhetoric, which was combative and condescending, did not help the cause. As one commentator put it, the protest became a movement among urbanites to restore their dignity in the face of PM's actions and words. Erdogan led the discursive counterattack on the protesters by calling them mere tools in the hands of "the interest lobby." In Erdogan's narrow usage of the phrase, the interest lobby simply refers to a group of national and international actors who strive to increase the fee on the loans given to Turkey. This phrase is not a new tool in Erdogan's rhetorical arsenal. Erdogan and his close circles, which include rising columnists and media tycoons, have repeatedly argued that his political and economic success has been at the expense of this lobby. Although finance capital is expected to seek higher returns, risk is the reverse side of the coin. Simply put, the interest rate by which a country borrows in international markets is determined by a plethora of risk factors such as local inflation rate, global economic prospects influencing the circulation of finance capital, and the debtor country's growth prospects and political stability signalling its ability to pay back loans. One cannot rule out foul play in international markets, though opportunistic behaviour cannot explain everything in the markets.

When the park was reopened on July 8 three weeks after the police had evicted the protesters, the Istanbul Governor Huseyin Avnni Mutlu announced that the park would be open for public use but protests would not be allowed.

> If certain groups claim to be the public and argue that "the park belongs to us, we are the owners of the park" we will not allow that.[16]

Implicit in this was the idea that the public should consist of conformist individuals who could be considered legitimate members of the public. Defining the parameters of public space and the limits of its inclusiveness is therefore significant. Political demonstrations do not conform to the governor's idea about the kind of function that a public sphere should serve so the protesters were excluded from the park. Similarly, Erdogan argued that the unrest was not reflective of the legitimate grievances of the Turks:

> The protests were nothing more than the minority's attempt to dominate the majority .... We could not have allowed this and we will not allow it ...[17]

In response hundreds of protesters stood outside the park and shouted "Everywhere is Taksim, Everywhere is Resistance."

The decision of the government to implement urban transformation through sudden top-down decisions that do not sufficiently account for environmental protection or consultation with citizens has been criticised as making the emergence of a consensus on the pace and nature of economic development difficult. The period of economic growth following the 2002 general elections led to major advances in Turkey's public services and infrastructure including airports, roads and highways, high-speed railroads, utilities, hospitals, universities and museums. In parallel vast process of urban transformation and renewal has taken place in many Turkish cities. Boosted by economic success and unchallenged political predominance the AKP government launched a number of initiatives the most emblematic of which were in or around Istanbul. Some were presented as indispensable for Turkey's economic growth like the third bridge over the Bosporus and a third airport for Istanbul. In undertaking these mega projects the government would not only have to take note of issues of sustainable development but also address legal considerations. This urban transformation was criticised both for the excessive centralisation of decision-making and the lack of consultation with citizens before projects were started.[18] In a number of instances there have been substantial amendments to legislative, regulatory and administrative frameworks for these projects. Attempts by civil societies to introduce local consultation mechanisms for urban transformation projects have been overlooked.

The current wave of urban transformation also has massive cultural and socio-economic effects. One consequence is the marginalisation of Istanbul's Roma people, an ethnic group that accounts for less than one per cent of Turkey's population. For instance, the Sulukule neighbourhood in Istanbul which has been historically inhabited by the Roma Communities was demolished to make way for a renovation project despite campaigns against the evictions. A 2012 report by the Open Society Foundation concluded that

> Evictions are about more than property, they interrupt the entire life, education, employment and progress of a family, possibly irreparably, and hasten the decline of the Roma people. Evictions must be viewed and addressed in this light.[19]

Another effect of urban modernisation is the development of new forms of wealth and poverty. "Gated" residential compounds have been introduced and the traditional temporary housing for recently arrived internal migrants (*gecekondu*) has been replaced by permanent marginal developments. Gentrification and marginalisation go hand in hand in Turkey and urban transformation, especially in Istanbul, has led to a form of social and spatial segregation of different groups.

It is not surprising that the issue of urban transformation has morphed into a nationwide political problem in Turkey. It is now the symbol of the country's disputed style of democratic management. The Taksim renovation project has become the symbol of the AKP's majoritarian concept of democracy. As Erdogan pointed out on June 7, 2013:

> We have said that we are going to demolish the AKM (the Ataturk Cultural Centre) on Taksim Square and build a huge opera house there. Participants of this vandalism immediately responded, "we won't let you demolish it." Excuse me, but we made this decision before elections and the majority of the people said "yes" for us in the elections. People supported us because they supported these projects.[20]

These statements have posed fundamental questions about the nature of democracy put forward by the AKP in terms of the ways in which the opinions, beliefs and lifestyles of half of the population who did not vote for the AKP has been disregarded. The rhetoric and symbolism generated by the protests brought to the forefront two interrelated aspects: on the one hand, it was about transforming interactions hitherto marked by social, cultural and emotional gaps; on the other, it was about imagining the possibility of a new progressive politics that could pose as an alternative. In other words, it was about whether a social movement would indeed be transformed into social change.

The Aftermath

On June 7, 2015, Turkey held general elections to elect 550 members of the Grand National Assembly and form the Twenty-Fifth Parliament. The election campaign had been marked by varying political agendas and marred by debates about the unlawful use of public funds by the ruling AKP, the state affiliated media's biased representations of the parties and President Erdogan's participation in the AKP's election rallies, despite a constitutional requirement for him to remain impartial. However, the principal pre-election issue remained whether the HDP could cross the 10 per cent threshold to enter Parliament. The results came as a reversal of the 13 years of domination of the AKP as a single-party government as the party failed to secure the 276 seats required to form a single-party government. The HDP managed to pass the 10% barrier, which reduced the number of seats in Parliament that would otherwise have gone to the AKP. The election results also thwarted President Erdogan's plans to change the country's Constitution and transform Turkey's parliamentary system into a presidential one. Erdogan had turned the June 2015 ballot into a kind of referendum towards his drive to rewrite the country's constitution, abolish parliamentarianism and instal a powerful new executive presidency occupied by himself. Since the AKP failed to get the required seats to form a majority government, the requirement was for a coalition government to be formed within 45 days to avoid a new election.

However, in the aftermath of the elections the AKP strategy was to block the formation of a coalition government and undermine future electoral prospects of the HDP with the hope that in the next polls the AKP would get a majority and therefore avoid the need for a coalition. Consequently all attempts at forming a coalition government failed and snap elections were called for. In the run-up to the elections there were attempts to repress the HDP's prospects and stoke nationalist sentiments to draw votes away from the MHP. Anti-Kurdish policies were renewed both domestically and in the neighbourhood. The Turkish government decided to extend assistance to the US air campaign against the Islamic State in Syria by opening the Incirlik airbase for use by US aircraft and by adding Turkish aircraft to the campaign. However, it was widely alleged that instead of striking Islamic State bases in Syria, Turkish warplanes targeted the PKK bases in Syria and Iraq. There was also large-scale detention of Kurdish politicians and activists within Turkey.

As the Turkish government increased its attacks on Kurdish forces there were predictably attacks on Turkish soldiers and police officers in the south-east and clashes between Kurdish militants and Turkish forces that left casualties on both sides. The result has been a campaign of violence that culminated in the bombings on a procession in Ankara on October 10 (subsequently blamed on the Islamic State) which was calling for resumption of peace talks between the PKK and the Turkish state. Recent attacks on the HDP, the PKK and the inevitable retaliation have been attempts to portray the idea of a "nation under threat" and encourage voters into supporting President Erdogan's security first agenda. Erdogan views parliamentary structures as constraining his ability to construct a super presidency. The justification for a change however has been couched in terms of an effective strong executive state more capable of facing terrorism, civil war, economic decline and corruption. In such circumstances freedom of the press is often the first casualty, and in the week leading up to the polls there was increasing pressure and takeover of the non-government media like *Bugun* and *Kanalturk TV* and dailies like *Bugun* and *Millet*. Similarly, Prime Minister Ahmet Davutuglu stressed what he referred to as a "terror cocktail" of the PKK, the Islamic State and the Revolutionary People's Liberation Party Front, all of whom wanted chaos in Turkey, thereby appealing to nationalist elements. The AKP election campaign for the November polls was based on the looming crisis and the slogan "after us there is chaos." And in this they were largely successful.

The AKP once again returned as the majority party with nearly 50% of the votes. Issues that dominated the debate were stability, security and employment opportunities in the face of an economy stretched to its limits by Syrian "guests." Democracy and protests seem to have taken a back seat. But, Istikkal Cadessi still bears traces of the graffiti that was drawn during the summer of 2013, and occasionally you can still hear groups gathering to sing a few protest songs. Apart from curious tourists, always on the move along one of Istanbul's most fashionable shopping streets, no one stops to listen. The heritage tram that moves from the Taksim side of the street towards Gezi operates as usual, blaring music. But in the course of a workshop on communication and social change, that takes place within the confines of the Swedish Research Institute, on the other end of the street from Gezi, there is a distinct impression that the protesters will wait for the next trigger to gather once again.

Notes

1. Gwilym Croucher, "Rethinking political symbolism: Government advertising and the 'Strengthening Medicare' campaign," Refereed paper presented to the Australasian Political Studies Association Conference, September 25-27, 2006, www.newcastle.edu.au/Resources/Schools/ Croucher-Gwilym
2. Murray J. Edelman, *The Symbolic Uses of Politics* (Urbana: University of Illinois, 1964).
3. While a flag has a literal meaning in that it designates a place and state it also connotes a variety of meanings about people, nation and governance. A national flag remains a pervasive and commonplace symbol of nationalism. While the notion of a nation is often that of an "imagined community" and it remains at least in part a mythical construct, the use of a flag permeates the national consciousness as a ubiquitous reference to the interests it exemplifies.
4. V. Turner, *The Forest of Symbols* (Ithaca: Cornell University Press, 1967).
5. Simon Harrison, "Four Types of Symbolic Conflict," *Journal of the Royal Anthropological Institute*, vol. 1, no. 2, 1995, p. 255.
6. Zyenap Gambetti, "The Gezi Resistance as Surplus Value," *Jadaliyya*, July 5, 2013.
7. From Jelle Rietveld, *The Capulcu of Gezi Park,* Istanbul 2013, citing a speech by Recep Tayyip Erdogan on June 2, 2013, jjrietveld.com/contemporary-art/the-capulcu-of-gezi-parki/
8. Nazan Ustundag, "Praise for the Marginal Groups," *Jadaliyya*, June 13, 2013.
9. Cited from "Turkey unrest: Unions call strike over crackdown," *BBC News Europe*, June 17, 2013.
10. "Judy Asks: Is Erdogan Finished?" *Carnegie Europe*, June 5, 2013.
11. For a detailed analysis see Bayram Balci, "Turkey: Local Elections Gave Huge Victory to Erdogan," *Foreign Policy Journal*, Op Ed, April 3, 2014.
12. Safak Bas, an analyst at the European Stability Initiative, Berlin, cited from "Turkey's Protests Indicate Growing Independence of Civil Society," *Eurasiareview, News and Analysis*, June 15, 2013.
13. Cited from a conversation reported in Thomas L. Friedman, "Postcard from Turkey," *New York Times, The Opinion Pages*, June 18, 2013.
14. From Hikmet Kocamaner, "Delinquent Kids, Revolutionary Mothers, Uncle Governor and Erdogan the Patriarch," Part One, *Jadaliyya*, August 5, 2013.
15. Pinar Melis Yelsali Parmaksiz, "#resistankara: Notes of Women Resisting," *Jadaliyya*, June 16, 2013.
16. Cited from James M. Dorsey, "Turkey Moves to Prevent Protests in Stadiums and on Campus," August 26, 2013, dennisloo.com/.../turkey-moves-to-prevent-protests-in-stadiums-and-on-.campus
17. Cited from "Turkey Unrest: Unions Call Strike Over Crackdown," *BBC News Europe*, June 17, 2013.
18. Marc Pierini, "Urban transformation in Turkey," *Carnegie Europe*, June 20, 2013.
19. Pierini, "Urban transformation in Turkey."
20. Pierini, "Urban transformation in Turkey."

Protest and the State

6. Gone with the Wind or a Tectonic Change? A Retrospective Analysis Based on the 2011 Israeli Socio-Political Protest Campaign

Tamar Hermann

Introduction

A massive socio-economic grassroots protest erupted in Israel in the summer of 2011. The initiators of this campaign, mostly young adults in their twenties and thirties, called for strategic changes in the government's social and economic policies, i.e., the reversal of the neoliberal economy. Their criticism focused on the high cost of living in general, and that of housing in particular, but beyond these, suggested a new approach to national priority scaling. In real time, public opinion polls indicated overwhelming support for the campaign as well as with its operative repertoire. Even among those public sectors which were not present in large numbers in the streets, a significant level of approval was recorded. Scepticism seemed to have left the stage free for hope.

And yet, much like other "Occupy Type" campaigns which emerged at about the same time in other countries, within a few months, the streets and town squares where most activity had taken place were empty, and the campaign lost momentum. The rapid decline of the campaign calls for special attention as no means of oppression, formal or informal, were used against it, neither by the government nor by other powerful social or political actors. Moreover, the key issues were not effectively addressed by decision-makers. In other words, very little if anything changed for the better, but still the campaign petered out. If this is not puzzling enough, then one should also note that in early 2013, and for the second time in March 2015, the ruling Likud party and the incumbent Prime Minister (Benjamin Netanyahu) won the national elections. These electoral achievements are especially challenging analytically, against the background of persistent socio-economic hardships and their permanent centrality in public discourse and the mass media. This state of affairs and climate of opinion were frequently acknowledged by top political figures from all parties. For example, in a programmatic speech made by Israeli President Reuven Rivlin in November 2014 at a gathering of top Israeli economic leaders, entrepreneurs and officials, the President maintained that too many Israelis felt disenfranchised and unable to fulfil their material and non-material needs. Although he did not use the specific term delegitimisation, in his speech the President stated categorically that the social contract between the Israeli citizens and the state had been breached. President Rivlin went so far as to state that this breach of contract jeopardised national security to the same extent as, if not more than, military unpreparedness for massive attacks from the outside.[1]

This article thus aims to examine why the 2011 Israeli socio-economic protest campaign dissipated. Another issue addressed is the balance sheet of the fulfilled and unfulfilled promises of the protest. Last but not least, an effort will be made to suggest some general insights regarding the potential effectiveness and resilience of such campaigns in democratic regimes in a globalised world.

The first part of this article will briefly present the central theoretical approaches to the emergence of political protest campaigns. The second part will describe the lifecycle of the 2011 Israeli socio-economic campaign. The third part will depict its four-year-old legacies and present certain assumptions regarding the potential of such campaigns to last and introduce significant changes in the political system.

What Drives People into the Streets?

Despite the emergence of a large number of protest events all over the world since the first decade of the 2000s,[2] including the mega "Arab Spring," from a theoretical point of view, only little analytical progress has been made thus far. Therefore, one still has to make do with the classical social/protest movement theories.[3]

The first-generation of contemporary grass-roots action scholarship, the mass behaviour theories, emerged in the 1950s and 1960s.[4] Their reading of collective behaviour was of accumulated irrational and emotional responses by alienated individuals. It dealt with the causes and formation of eruptions of citizen discontent, which, influenced by the painful memories of the totalitarian–communist and fascist—experience, were viewed as a severe threat to the stability and proper functioning of democratic regimes. The basic hypothesis of these theories was that people would protest when deprived of the (mostly material) assets to which they felt they were entitled. Yet, in reality, we know that the man in the street often gets involved in political protest not only when hungry or disenfranchised but also, for example, when feeling relatively deprived compared to "others" in terms of recognition, identity and the like.[5] Furthermore, as the "new" social movement phenomenon suggests, participants in many such contemporary citizens' campaigns—human rights activists, environmentalists, or anti-globalists—do not have a more personal stake in the causes they pursue than do other members of the same political collective. Thus, self-interest alone which was so highly stressed by the mass behaviour school does not serve as a satisfying explanation for all sorts of grass-roots participation.

Second-generation theories therefore addressed a different research agenda: what is needed for grass-roots movements to gain momentum and achieve their goals? These theories, often referred to as the Resource Mobilisation School, mainly proposed that the availability and allocation of human and material resources determine the campaign's mobilisation capabilities and practical outcomes. This postulate diverted scholarly attention away from the reasons for the protest, to the social movement organisation (SMO): its internal and external networking, decision-making routines, mobilisation techniques and lifecycle.[6]

Social movement/protest theory did not remain fixed in the Resource Mobilisation phase. Another conceptual framework, the Political Opportunity Structure (POS), was developed in the 1970s.[7] The Political Process framework, the theoretical framework of the POS, emerged in the late 1970s and early 1980s.[8]

The POS concept suggests that social movements emerge in response to specific circumstances, and not necessarily to the level of frustration or the human and material resources available for the movement or its networking skills. The core notion of POS is the set of environmental elements that catalyse movements, translating the potential for collective action into actual mobilisation. In other words, according to Political Process theoreticians, for a social movement, the "when"—when the POS is "ripe"—goes a long way towards explaining the "why"—why people get politically involved in this way. The POS concept also helps to understand when a social movement is able to gain access into the political system and how and when it is more likely to evaporate at a very early stage, leaving no traces behind. The questions addressed here were why social movements emerge or decline when they do, and why they take different trajectories. The basic answer was that "[c]hanging opportunities help explain why movements emerge at one point in time rather than another, and differences in political opportunities help explain why movements are successful in some countries or regions and not in others."[9]

The POS represents "consistent but not necessarily formal or permanent national dimensions of the political environment which either encourage or discourage people from using collective action."[10] A favourable POS, it was maintained, arises more sporadically than grievances and organisational resources, yet exerts a far more critical influence on a movement's prospects. In practice, it even determines the movement's resource mobilisation abilities,[11] structure,[12] and behaviour.[13]

McAdam, McCarthy, and Zald[14] list four dimensions of POS on which almost all studies within this analytical framework rest:

- Level of openness of the institutionalised political system
- Level of stability of the elite alignments
- Existence of allies within the elite
- The state's capacity and propensity for repression.

Naturally, the POS changes with time, thereby changing the movement's mobilisation potential, its strategies and its potential and actual achievements. A change in the POS would be the result, for example, of the reshuffling of global or regional structures, electoral realignments, divisions among elites, or the emergence or disappearance of influential allies within the political establishment. Empirical studies point to the possibility of POS expansion, i.e., making it more conducive to the movement's purposes,[15] its contraction,[16] and even the possibility of simultaneous expansion and contraction.[17]

In order to increase the chances of the movement's success, its activists need to thoroughly explore the specific POS within which they operate, as "the structures of everyday life may ultimately be changed by collective action, but in the short run they are relatively fixed, and serve as the relational underpinning for most collective action."[18]

Popular as they have become, POS theories seem to be facing growing criticism. The most common criticism concerns POS as an ex post facto analytical tool—successes or failures are explained only in retrospect, as the result of an expanded or contracted POS.[19] A second stream of criticism holds that POS theories paid little attention to changes in the technical facilities available to the movements. One clear example of such a change is the emergence of Computer-Mediated Communication (CMC) which was ignored in POS theories though it dramatically increases the operational abilities of social movements. Technology operates as a powerful facilitator for social activism through the development of cultural and "socio-spatial 'enclaves,'"[20] and hence represent a major facilitator of grass-roots activity. The defenders of classical POS definitions would argue that the contribution of CMC to the creation of new types of communities and the spread of new democratic practices is not yet clear. Yet, it appears that technical improvements are more critical to social activism than original POS theoreticians were ready to assume. The third line of criticism argues that POS theoreticians have focused too much on the practical manifestations while neglecting central issues such as ideology, culture, identity and emotions.

This last critique produced the notion of "framing" as another tool for analysing social movement activity. Framing is commonly defined as "conscious strategic efforts by groups of people to fashion shared understandings of the world and of themselves that legitimate and motivate collective actions."[21] The complimentary notion to framing is "resonance"—the extent to which the way the movement frames the problem is accepted by its audience and sustains its mobilisation efforts. It is worth mentioning that, in most cases, the proponents of framing theories did not aspire to create a new school of thought on social movements but only to enrich the theory so that it includes more than the study of POS and strategies of resource mobilisation. Framing is actually meant to amalgamate earlier social movement theories: "mediating between opportunity, organisation and action, are the shared meanings and definitions that people bring to this situation."[22]

The following analysis of the 2011 Israeli case will mostly rely on POS theory with some references to the notion of framing.

"The People Demand Social Justice!"

On July 14, 2011, the French nation, and many other people around the globe, joyfully celebrated the 222nd anniversary of the French revolution. On the very same date, a seething undercurrent of socio-economic dissatisfaction erupted in Israel, taking the shape of a massive grass-roots street protest campaign.[23] Obviously the two events were not comparable in significance, magnitude or consequences. The French revolution changed the way people are governed worldwide while the Israeli protest of summer 2011 was confined to a small country and even there—at least thus far—left the political superstructure pretty much intact. Yet it is appropriate to mention the two events together because the legacy of the former shaped, in some important respects, the latter's agenda and expectations.

Indeed, it was not only the French revolution which served as the ideological role model for the Israeli anti-government campaign. Contemporaneous events in other countries also served as examples. After a number of years in which street protests seemed to have lost their allure and efficacy worldwide, the end of the first decade of the 2000s saw massive outbreaks of social unrest in the US, Spain, Chile, Greece and other places,[24] including those right around the corner from Tel Aviv, in Cairo's Tahrir Square and in other Arab countries, initially referred to as the "Arab Spring."

The notion of the people as the ultimate sovereign in a democratic regime, which was widely spread by the French revolution and other democratic revolutions, was reflected in 2011 Israel by the leading slogan: "The people demand social justice!" No specification however was put forward (nor asked for) at the time regarding the question of who the relevant "people" were in terms of their national, social and demographic characteristics. Nor was the notion of "social justice" elaborated. This was intentional. The organisers wished this ambiguity to be a tool for expanding the relevant audiences of the campaign's message. However, soon enough, as could have been forecast based on the framing school's postulates, this strategic choice proved unconstructive. Ambiguity was one of the reasons for the rapid development of internal cleavages among the protesters as well as within the leading core group; for example, it turned out that middle class protesters' understanding of the term "social justice" was not identical in the best case, and perhaps even orthogonal, to its framing by the protesting weaker social strata and their representatives.

In each country, the reasons and triggers for the upsurge in people's discontent in and after 2010 were somewhat different. However, the common thread between all these endeavours can be traced back to the French revolution which gave birth and meaning to the new notion of citizenship and invested it with a list of rights. It also gave credence to initiating a grass-roots revolt against legitimate rulers who had not proven themselves accountable and attentive to the sovereign body—the people. Admittedly, neither the French Revolution nor the Egyptian Tahrir Square uprising were openly acknowledged in Israel 2011 as relevant precedents; nevertheless, their democratic legacy served as a "cognitive frame" for this local undertaking.

It is not by chance that July 14, not a day before or a day after, was the date selected by the initiator of the Israeli endeavour, a young middle-class Israeli woman, Daphne Leef, a film editor in her late twenties, to put out a call via Facebook to friends and colleagues to join her in the tent she set up on Rothschild Boulevard, one of the main streets of Tel Aviv, in protest of the cost of housing. In her call, she framed her personal housing problems, mainly skyrocketing rent, as a general malaise.[25] The impact of CMC (in this case, Facebook) proved beyond anyone's expectations. Much to the amazement of Leef herself, not to mention Israel's upper political and economic echelons, who allowed themselves to dismiss earlier manifestations of public dissatisfaction, Leef's message—the rising cost of living in Israel and the government's inattentiveness—strongly resonated in the ears of hundreds, then thousands, and, at its peak, hundreds of thousands of Israelis, mainly between the ages of 25 and 35. Within 24 hours, many translated their sympathy with Leef's message into action, and came to the boulevard, at first in most cases for a short stay only, but which, for several thousand participants, developed into an almost three-month-long street vigil.

In no time, the expanding tent camp developed a culture of dialogue and body language which was heavily influenced by parallel campaigns in other countries, mainly by the Spanish anti-austerity "indignados" movement. Dialogue circles were organised day and night, and thousands of Israelis came from all over the country to take part in these discussions on the citizens' problems and the government's inefficacy to deal with them, or even just to watch and express their support for the new endeavour. Nearby restaurants supplied the protesters with free food and people residing in neighbouring parts of the city opened their doors to the protesters' for a shower or laundry. An unprecedented and indeed unexpected sense of camaraderie and solidarity emerged in the camp as well as outside it, bridging— even if only for a short time—the existing social and economic cleavages. Young and old, poor and rich, men and women, liberal and more conservative seemed, at the beginning, to be united in their joint demand for the unspecified "social justice."

The national media coverage of the protest and its core leaders was both intensive and positive from the very first moment. In particular, it was openly supported by one of the three main Israeli financial newspapers, *The Marker*, which both helped shape and echoed the campaign's demands. This exposure had its pros and cons: on the one hand, it offered the protest leaders a convenient platform to disseminate their message. On the other hand, it put a very heavy burden on their shoulders by reflecting and magnifying their inexperience as well as the emerging internal strategic and tactic disagreements. Also, the many media visuals of the quite relaxed, often untidy and not properly dressed tent-camp dwellers projected the image of a local, non-violent Woodstock style endeavour, rather than of an emerging revolutionary vanguard. Moreover, the almost unreserved initial support by the media boomeranged when the campaign declined as the formerly emphatic and then disappointed and frustrated journalists turned their backs on the campaign's leadership declaring it to be a total failure, thereby fostering a similar public perception of the campaign's balance sheet.

Going back to the beginning of the campaign, it seems that Leef's initial call was timely and to the point. The combination of frustration and the desire to make a significant change in the national priority scale apparently touched a very sensitive note in the Israeli public's heart and mind. In terms of the POS theory presented above, the already open national structure expanded even further. Political protest was considered highly legitimate; many political and civil bodies serve as the sustaining social network and the state was reluctant to use any means of oppression. Like in many other Western states at that time, it was the middle classes and their particular needs, demands and expectations which stood at the centre of the protest agenda. In Israel, too, the middle classes that since the 1960s had become accustomed to an ever-rising standard of living, felt the earth shaking beneath their feet as their economic situation seemed to deteriorate and their future, rather bleak. The centrality of these specific concerns, which were not acknowledged as such, reduced the "people" and their demand for "justice" to a class interest. Hence, within a few days, the weaker social strata, expecting to get a voice in the campaign as well, began to feel marginalised and therefore frustrated and angry, and many deserted the camps—if they had a place to which to return ...

It must be stressed, however, that when the protest campaign began, Israel's national macro-economic indicators were (and still are) impressively positive. According to the standard indicators, the Israeli economy was doing well while other developed and developing countries where protests gained momentum at the same time were struggling with the dismal economic consequences of the post-2008 meltdown. For example, the level of unemployment in Israel in 2011 was only about 7%, the national deficit was reasonable by common standards and the GNP per capita was up to around $31,000. The national growth rate of the economy was also promising: over 4.5%. And yet, inequality and income gaps had become more and more apparent and the sense of relative deprivation had deepened. The latter was fuelled by a growing awareness—mainly among middle-class, secular, urban, educated and employed Israelis in their late twenties, thirties and early forties—that not only had the cost of living become higher than their income, but that the prospect of closing this gap in the foreseeable future was minimal. The burning issues were, thus, housing costs, gas, and food (the price increase of the popular cottage cheese symbolically turned into one of the main areas of conflict). These young people, who, in due course, comprised the backbone of the various protest events, realised that, for the first time in the state's relatively short history, as an age cohort they would do worse economically than their parents' generation.[26] Thus, for example, for members of the middle-class younger generation, the chances of buying an apartment in the central part of the country were close to nil, while almost all members of their parents' generation had "made" it. The discrepancy between the objective positive macro indicators presented by the government as evidence of its successful policies, and the subjective sense of facing an economic dead end, was the main catalyst for the eruption of the protest.

The 2011 campaign should not be understood only against the background of the economic state of affairs, but also against that of the prevalent sense of robust national security which allowed public attention to turn away from the military and foreign affairs that normally dominate Israeli political discourse. Hence, despite the deadlock in the Israeli-Palestinian negotiations and the prevalent perception that peace was nowhere on the horizon, the sense was that national security was in good shape. In other words, whereas in times of active external conflict, Israelis do not allow themselves to focus on domestic problems, the current situation provided a window of opportunity for socio-economic issues to be brought to the fore. Theories describe such a situation as an "open structure of political opportunities."

A third factor that should be mentioned here in order to shed light on the specific timing of the protest was the mounting level of mistrust in the political system which characterised the national climate of opinion at that time. The public sense of confidence in the decency and efficacy of the political system and national leaders hit rock bottom in the early 2010s. Many corruption cases were exposed and the unholy alliance between top politicians and tycoons was frequently on the table or even taken to the courts. Also, as far as the political background is concerned, in 2011 the Israeli left was already in shambles in terms of its public appeal and could barely offer support to the protest campaign without "contaminating" its image. Right-wing political bodies, however, were antagonistic toward the campaign as they considered it a camouflage for a leftist political effort to topple the Likud government.

Together with the widening gaps between those who had and those who had not, these issues caused thousands of Israelis to openly and publicly identify with Leef and her colleagues' list of demands: Replacing the government's neoliberal orientation and policies with a social-democratic agenda—that is, lower state-regulated rents, subsidised public housing, reduced food and gas prices, heavier taxation on "tycoons" and large corporations, increased state investments in welfare, schooling and health, etc.

Following the Rothschild tent camp example, other smaller tent camps appeared in various parts of Tel Aviv as well as in other cities and towns (including Arab ones), including in Jerusalem, the capital of Israel. However they all remained secondary to the main camp and received little media attention. Six days after Leef's tent was set up in the boulevard (July 23, 2011) the first massive rally was organised. People from all over the country assembled in Tel Aviv as well as in smaller parallel gatherings in other parts of the country. The total number of protesters nationwide was estimated by the police to be around 85,000, a fairly promising indication of relevance. The main concrete demand raised by the various speakers in the main rally and echoed elsewhere was to drastically change the government's attention and budget allocation in a way which would enable it to deal effectively with the skyrocketing cost of living as well as to reduce the widening socio-economic gaps. Public support for the protest right at the beginning and admittedly even when everyone already went back home was high, as shown in the graph below.[27] According to various research projects and public opinion surveys, a world record of around 25% of the population took part in one or more of the 2011 activities!

At the following stage, as the protest gained momentum, its leaders had to make certain strategic decisions regarding their message, audiences and partners. The message, it was agreed, would target first and foremost the neoliberal economy fostered by the government and its repercussions. With the assistance of marketing PR experts who offered their services at no charge, the desired social justice for the people was framed as standing in stark contradiction to neoliberalism, and compatible with the social-democratic creed. This message fit the average Israeli's gut feelings and the country's social and economic legacies.[28] From this point of view, our case study went hand in hand with the assertion of the resource mobilisation theory that the chances of a protest movement taking off and achieving its aims are significantly improved if its message resembles ideological precedents.

Yet, as mentioned earlier, the practical interpretation of these legacies and sentiments were not shared by all participants in the campaign. A minor but indicative example of the disagreements which emerged in the later stages of the campaign involved a generation gap. Thus, while younger middle-class participants wished to see state regulation imposed on their landlords so that their rent could not be raised arbitrarily and often, their parents' age cohort, who had quite often invested their life savings in apartments for rent in order to maintain their standard of living after they retired, were reluctant to see rent regulated by the state. Even more detrimental were the conflicts of interest between the middle class and the lower class, which rose to the surface when efforts were made to write an economic platform. However, none of these conflicts were openly acknowledged or tackled.

As already mentioned in brief, in order to bring as many Israelis as possible on board, the organisers of the campaign adopted an "apolitical"[29] posture. In fact, this was an empty slogan: their endeavour may have been non-partisan but certainly was not apolitical because their main concern was to change allocation of national resources, an inherently political mission. This apolitical façade was shortly challenged by opponents within and outside of the government and in the eyes of more than a few, cast some doubt as to the campaign organisers' integrity. Still, in the context of their up to the last moment apolitical frontage, the Rothschild tent camp leaders—who were almost immediately selected by the media to function as the faces of the campaign—decided not to give a foothold or to allow any political party to get involved, let alone take ownership of their undertaking. They refused to be assisted financially or strategically by any politically-coloured bodies. Thus they declined an offer made by the chairperson of the largest workers' union (*Histadrut*)[30] to bring his multi-member organisation on board.[31] They did, however, join forces with the Israeli Student Union, and its chairperson, Itzik Shmuli, became one of the top campaign figures.[32] They also opened the door to cooperation with certain liberal NGOs, such as the—much left of centre—New Israel Fund, a partnership which again made their apolitical self-definition doubtful in the eyes of many.

The authenticity of the manifested apolitical nature of the protest was also questioned based on the socio-demographic and socio-political composition of its leaders and the body of protesters.[33] In tent camps other than the main one on Rothschild Boulevard, protesters from a diverse range of ethnic, socio-economic, national and ideological backgrounds were present. Yet the core group of leaders remained rather homogeneous; they were mostly Ashkenazi Jews, secular, well educated, urban and middle class. No representative of other societal groups was invited to join this vanguard. Furthermore, the participants in the large rallies (July 23, August 23, September 3) and even more so their leaders, represented a small range of political preferences: centre and left of centre. This composition was not a secret and almost immediately, by way of elimination, alienated certain public sectors from the protest: voters of the hard-core parties of the right, the orthodox and the ultra-orthodox communities, West Bank settlers, who are mostly right-wing and orthodox, the non-Ashkenazi social periphery, less economically prosperous social peripheries, etc. Relative newcomers from the former Soviet Union were also under-represented in the campaign since, based on their past experience, they tended to perceive street protest as a risky tactic for political resistance. Initially, the Israeli Arab community showed noticeable signs of interest in taking part in the protest. However, the Jewish organisers were not too keen on having them on board as their presence in great numbers could have estranged the Jewish majority. Furthermore, Arab participants, let alone partners to the strategy-making, would have necessitated some mention of the Israeli occupation of the Palestinian territories. However, in the context of the apoliticisation strategy, no mention was ever made of the occupation. Ex post facto, however, in the eyes of campaign critics, avoidance of this "elephant in the room" undermined the campaign's potential for developing into a mature social movement.

Its shortcomings notwithstanding, at the time, the protest injected a high dose of hope into Israeli public discourse and indeed created some sense of urgency at the political top. In order to display attentiveness to the campaign demands, on August 8, 2011, Prime Minister Netanyahu announced the appointment of a special commission, headed by a widely respected Economics professor (Manuel Trajtenberg). The commission was tasked with coming up with proposals on how to change priorities in order to lighten the load of the Israeli citizen, implement a new taxation system, provide better access to social services, increase competition in the Israeli economy, and suggest actual measures that needed to be taken to reduce housing prices.

Meanwhile the campaign suffered several setbacks: the leaders were openly challenged as not being representative enough and not asking nor getting a mandate from the various tent camps to speak and negotiate on their behalf. Within the core group, ideological rifts between moderates and radicals eroded its ability to translate the initial momentum and solidarity into a full-fledged political strategy, let alone come up with a blueprint for dealing with socio-economic difficulties. Certain members took the easy way out and stated that it was the government's role, not theirs, to work out solutions, while others maintained that they should put forward at least an alternative list of recommendations to that of the Trajtenberg Commission. Another internal controversy had to do with the question of whether the mass rallies should or should not end with singing the national anthem: while certain leaders resented this idea for political reasons, others maintained that they would call off the rally if the anthem were not sung because omission of the anthem would boomerang as a non-patriotic statement. There were also struggles over the campaign's top leading position, as so often happens in social endeavours with no clear leader selection rules. Finally, the initial attraction of the protest gradually evaporated and the tent camps lost their early positive atmosphere. The neighbours started to resent the camp's presence and the municipalities worried because of the massive accumulation of leftover food and other garbage and of the arrival of some problematic social elements—homeless, drunk, drug abusers and mentally unstable individuals. Rumours of some unreported rape cases were also in the air.

The campaign ended in practice with a crescendo: a rally of 400,000 people in Tel Aviv in early September, just before the beginning of the academic year and the Jewish high holidays. Shortly afterwards, the tent camps disappeared; the only tents left belonged almost only to those who had nowhere else to go. These were dismantled by the local municipalities in blitz operations, which in certain cases involved significant force against the few remaining protesters. The leadership group also fell apart; some very frustrated members totally abandoned the public sphere, others opted for social activism and a few turned to conventional party politics. In practice, only the media and, to a greater extent, academia, were left to reflect and produce a variety of balance sheets.

What Went Right and What Went Wrong?

Downsides

The mixed feelings toward the 2011 protest are the result of the fact that it did not meet the expectations of its participants and supporters in three very important respects:

1. *Short Lifespan*

Protest waves are known for their short lifespan. In most cases they come and go in days, weeks, or, at most, months. Sometimes they reappear a few months or several years later. This is why certain social movement analysts compare their behaviour pattern to a whale swimming—above and below the surface of the sea (Young, 1986). Only if the campaign develops a clear agenda and strategic blueprint, manages to mobilise the critical resources, and is not intercepted immediately by the state, can it survive longer. The 2011 Israeli protest did not meet these minimal thresholds. Summer in Israel is good for spending time outdoors and for organising massive street rallies. This turned out to be even more tempting as for a couple of months the Tel Aviv municipality provided the tent camp with heavy-duty cleaning services, and as mentioned, the immediate surroundings were highly supportive. In a way then, it was the (too) convenient circumstances that prevented the protest from experiencing friction with its neighbours which, according to "PoS" (Product of Sums) theory, is necessary to keep the protest going. Another reason for the campaign's short lifespan was the fact that its leaders' inner circle was split. With no leaders and few followers around, it is clear why, for all practical purposes, the campaign dissipated, leaving behind a bitter taste.

2. *Internal Conflicts*

The point of departure of the 2011 protest was that it was a campaign of "the people against the government." Based on this position, efforts were made to create comprehensive grass-roots solidarity or at least an agreed-upon list of demands. However, within a few weeks, it became clear that the socio-economic interests of the various public sectors which were allegedly represented by the campaign were far from complementary. For example, the Jewish Israeli protesters defined their interests and goals in an essentially different way than Israeli Arabs who felt unwelcome. Similar conflicts of interest developed between the so-called (Jewish) centre and the periphery, between the middle class and the blue collar workers, between those settlers who were interested in joining the lines and the protest leaders who, on an individual level, belonged to the political left, although they acted as if this was an apolitical game, and so on. A generation gap also became apparent between the middle-aged members of the middle class and the generation of the renters, who depicted them as greedy. In a short while, thus, it turned out that more than being "the people against the government," the real conflict was among the people. With a narrow solidarity base and few shared interests, the chances for any campaign to stay alive were meagre, and this one was no exception.

3. *Ideological Ambiguity*

In their effort to bring as many people as possible on board, the young and inexperienced leaders of the campaign tried to make do with focusing on the government deficiencies alone, without suggesting any solutions to the weighty economic dilemmas which they themselves raised. Efforts by more experienced, often older, activists and experts to persuade them that such a posture was strategically self-defeating fell on deaf ears.

Indeed, the desire to be acknowledged as apolitical and the refusal to offer detailed solutions to the problems they raised were not very convincing. Thus, their social rhetoric looked "pinkish" in the eyes of many, particularly as the endeavour was hailed and supported by many intellectuals and academics known for their socialist ideology. Once the protest was tainted with this political colour, large parts of the Israeli public became alienated from it, and so were, of course, those whose interests would have been jeopardised if the protest goals had been achieved, from the very rich oligarchs to the middle-class owners of one or two rental apartments. On the other hand, the radical left-wing activists saw the ambiguous world view put forward by the protest leaders as an indication of their lack of commitment and perhaps even as a cover-up for a bourgeois mentality. Either way, the professed ideological ambiguity boomeranged and, at the end of the day, proved counterproductive.

The above three drawbacks notwithstanding, the 2011 protest had some significant achievements, which have significantly improved Israeli democracy.

Achievements

1. *Reviewing the National Priority Scale*

Involved since its independence in a protracted conflict, military/security-related issues have always been Israel's top priority. As various research projects have shown, in certain respects, the Israeli public is constantly rallying around the flag. The siege mentality of both the nation's leaders and the public has limited the ability to direct national attention to other matters. The same goes for the budget allocation which has always been heavily subjugated to security needs. Therefore, previous efforts by socially-oriented actors from within or from outside the political establishment to divert more attention or more resources to reduce the widening socio-economic gap have failed miserably. One of the main demands of the 2011 protest rallies was to cater more to the economic needs of the people, even if this was at the expense of the security budget. The public was extremely attentive to and supportive of these demands: a month after the campaign started, 78% of Israeli-Jewish respondents in a public opinion survey agreed that a financial reallocation in favour of the social issues should be made and 53% agreed that money should be taken from the security budget for that purpose.[34] Despite the dissipation of the protest after only 2 months, this new civic orientation has proved long-lasting. Almost three years later, in April 2014, 47% of Israeli-Jewish respondents mentioned reduction of the socio-economic gaps as the main target for the government to pursue and another 21% noted that the creation of affordable housing solutions was a main goal (together this totalled 68%). Only 10% topped their list with the strengthening of Israel's military capabilities and another 9% with reaching a peace agreement with the Palestinians (altogether 19%).[35]

This new set of priorities was clearly manifested in the agenda of the 2013 and 2015 national elections. Another indication was the unexpected electoral achievements in 2013 and, to some extent, in 2015 of parties that devoted much attention in their electoral messages to economic and social issues directly addressing the concerns of younger middle-class voters. In addition, in the wake of the protest and in line with its young spirit, the average age of Israeli parliamentarians dropped; several leaders of the protest campaign were themselves elected Members of Knesset, thus politically mainstreaming the protest demands. Last but not least, there are empirical indications that political involvement of the younger age cohorts in both national and local politics and in social activism increased significantly in the wake of the 2011 experience.

2. *Promoting Transparency and Accountability*

The word accountability does not have a Hebrew equivalent. Some argue that this linguistic lacuna reflects a democratic deficiency in the national political culture—the elected representatives, let alone appointed office holders, simply do not feel accountable to their constituencies. Admittedly, for years, the public accepted this state of affairs as a given. The existing electoral system, in which the entire country is one district, contributed significantly to this deficiency. As mentioned above, the protest leaders did not call for structural change in the system. However, they often addressed the urgent need for accountability and transparency and democratic values. This instigated a serious debate about the right of the people in a democracy to be informed about decision-making processes and to gain open access to various official data. And indeed, subsequently, various steps were taken in that direction, including the establishment of the Open Knesset workshop,[36] and the government's formal decision to join the Open Government International Initiative.

In addition, the demand for accountability and transparency was supported by the media, which gave it very positive coverage. The alliance with the media helped to spread these notions and to integrate them into the public discourse. As a result, in recent years, Israel has witnessed an avalanche of exposures of unacceptable connections between politicians and political bodies and various corporations and tycoons, which often end up in court.

Some Conclusions

The 2011 protest did not succeed in bringing about the social and economic change it aspired to. The painful descent from the euphoria of mid-July 2011 to the bitter disappointment following mid-September indeed left a somewhat discouraging legacy regarding the ability of grass-roots campaigns to transform the political system. However, in retrospect, it appears that, in the wake of the campaign, several important changes for the better were introduced into the Israeli democratic culture: it injected new blood and new ideas into national political discourse, legitimised a change in national priorities and politicised new and younger people. It also created an unprecedented alliance between the media and social activists, and forced the government to open up to wider and deeper public scrutiny. Admittedly, this is not enough, but it certainly brought Israeli democracy to a better place and may serve in the future as a springboard for further improvements.

On the more general level, this case study suggests several insights which should be further explored in the future: First, that even apparently failed protest endeavours can leave positive legacies. Second, it opens the door to the idea of unacknowledged "spillover": apparently because of the protracted hostility between Israel and its neighbours, Israeli protesters never admitted to being influenced by the Arab Spring message. However, the similarity in timing, tactics and demands suggest that the 2011 campaign was part of a regional grass-roots political awakening. Finally, it seems that in order to come up with a good explanatory study of the balance sheet of a protest campaign, bits and pieces of all three schools—resource mobilisation theory, POS and framing theory—are needed, as none is sufficient by itself.

Notes

1. President Rivlin's speech was given on November 3, 2015, at the Eli Hurvitz Conference on Economy and Society, Haifa, Israel.
2. P. Norris, S. Walgrave and P. Van Aelst, "Who Demonstrates? Antistate Rebels, Conventional Participants, or Everyone?" *Comparative Politics* (PhD Programme in Political Science of the City University of New York) 2005, 37 (2): 189-205.
3. This part of the article summarises the theoretical section in Hermann, 2009, pp. 14-28.

4. W. Kornhauser, *The Politics of Mass Society*. (New York: The Free Press, 1959); N. Smelser, *The Theory of Collective Behaviour* (New York: The Free Press, 1962).
5. T. R. Gurr, *Why Men Rebel* (Princeton, NJ: Princeton University Press, 1970).
6. M. N. Zald and R. Ash, "Social Movement Organizations: Growth, Decay, and Change," in *Social Forces,* 1966, 44:327-41; J. D. McCarthy and M. N. Zald, 1977, "Resource Mobilization and Social Movements: A Partial Theory," in *American Journal of Sociology* 82(6):1212-41; D. McAdam, J. D. McCarthy and M. N. Zald (eds.), *Comparative Perspectives on Social Movements: Political Opportunities, Mobilizing Structures, and Cultural Framings* (New York: Cambridge University Press, 1996).
7. P. K. Eisinger, "The Conditions of Protest Behaviour in American Cities," in *American Political Science Review* 1973, 67:11-28.
8. C. Tilly, *From Mobilization to Revolution* (Reading, MA: Addison-Wesley, 1978).
9. B. Klandermans, and S. Staggenborg, "Introduction" in *Methods of Social Movement Research*, edited by B. Klandermans and S. Staggenborg, ix-xx (Minneapolis: University of Minnesota Press, 2002), xi.
10. Sidney Tarrow, "Power in Movement. Social Movements, Collective Action and Politics" (Cambridge and New York: Cambridge University Press, 1994), p. 18.
11. H. P. Kitschelt, "Political Opportunity Structures and Political Protest: Anti-Nuclear Movements in Four Democracies," in *British Journal of Political Science* 16, 1986, (1):57-86.
12. S. Tarrow, "States and Opportunities: The Political Structuring of Social Movements," in McAdam, McCarthy and Zald (eds.), *Comparative Perspectives on Social Movements* ..., pp. 41-61.
13. D. Della Porta, "Political Protest, Protesters, and Protest Policing: Public Discourse in Italy and Germany from the 1960s to the 1980s," in M. Giugni, D. McAdam and C. Tilly (eds.), *How Social Movements Matter* (Minneapolis: University of Minnesota Press, 1999), pp. 66-96.
14. D. McAdam, J. D. McCarthy and M. N. Zald (eds.), *Comparative Perspectives on Social Movements ...,* p. 10.
15. M. Goldner, "Expanding Political Opportunities and Changing Collective Identities in the Complementary and Alternative Medicine Movement," in P. G. Coy (ed.), *Political Opportunities, Social Movements and Democratization* (Oxford: Elsevier/JAI, 2001), pp. 69-102.
16. A. Melucci, "The Process of Collective Identity," in H. Johnston and B. Klandermans (eds.), *Social Movements and Culture* (Minneapolis: University of Minnesota Press, 1995), pp. 41-63.
17. D. Suh, "How Do Political Opportunities Matter for Social Movements: Political Opportunity, Misframing, Pseudosuccess, and Pseudofailure," in *The Sociological Quarterly* 42, 2001. (3):437-60.
18. J. D. McCarthy, "Constraints and Opportunities in Adopting, Adapting and Inventing," in McAdam, McCarthy and Zald (eds.), *Comparative Perspectives on Social Movement ...,* p. 147.
19. D. S. Meyer and D. Minkoff, "Conceptualizing Political Opportunity," in *Social Forces* 82, 2004 (4):1457-92.
20. C. Calhoun, "Community without Propinquity Revisited: Communications Technology and the Transformation of the Urban Public Sphere," in *Sociological Inquiry* 68, 1998 (3):383-84.

21. D. A. Snow, R. D. Benford et al., "Ideology, Frame Resonance and Participant Mobilization," in B. Klandermans, H. Kriesi, and S. Tarrow (eds.), *From Structure to Action: Comparing Social Movement Research across Cultures* (Greenwich, CT: JAI Press, 1988), p. xx.
22. D. McAdam, J. D. McCarthy and M. N. Zald, *Comparative Perspectives on Social Movements* ..., p. 5.
23. This dissatisfaction had been manifested in the early months of 2011 in a series of strikes (e.g., social workers, physicians) as well as in several consumer protests against the high prices of certain basic goods (mainly cottage cheese and gas).
24. L. Grinberg, "Comparing Occupy Movements: Global Mobilizing Power, Local Political Context and Dynamic," XVIII ISA World Congress, Yokohama, Japan, July 13-19, 2014.
25. Z. Rosenhek, and M. Shalev, "The Political Economy of Israel's 'Social Justice' Protests: A Class and Generational Analysis." *Contemporary Social Science: Journal of the Academy of Social Sciences*, 2013. http://dx.doi.org/10.1080/21582041.2013.851405. Later, the campaign's agenda was expanded to include other social and economic problems.
26. Rosenhek & Shalev, ibid.
27. The monthly figures in the graph are taken from the Peace Index surveys. See www.peaceindex.org. with the April 2014 figures taken from the *Israeli Democracy Index 2014*.
28. Most Israelis identify with the social-democratic world view, e.g. Hermann et al. 2014, 16. http://en.idi.org.il/media/3823043/democracy_index_2014_Eng.pdf
29. This "apolitical" façade was not unique to the Israeli endeavour; see, for example, Burnham (2001), Wood & Flinders (2014).
30. The *Histadrut* is politically associated with the Labour Party.
31. Later, some reporters exposed the fact that the campaign was financially assisted (although not initiated or guided) by certain supportive businessmen, one of whom even provided the campaign leaders with office space and services in Tel Aviv near the tent camp.
32. When the campaign dissolved, Shmuli and another (female) leader, Stav Shafir, gave up on grass-roots activism and accepted the invitation to join the Labour Party list for the 2013 elections, and became members of the Israeli parliament (Knesset).
33. A. Rotman, M. Shalev and Y. Shavit, "Where Did the Protest Come From? A Spatial and Political Analysis of Israel's 2011 Social Protest." Draft paper for the Reclaiming the City Square workshop, Tel Aviv University, April 2014.
34. August 2011 Peace Index Survey. http://www.peaceindex.org/newsletterEng.aspx?year=2011&month=8
35. April 2014 Peace Index Survey. http://www.peaceindex.org/indexMonthEng.aspx?num=274&monthname=April#.U579l_mSxqU
36. http://www.hasadna.org.il/en/our-projects/open-knesset/

Bibliography

Burnham, P. 2001. New Labour and the Politics of Depoliticisation. *British Journal of Politics and International Relations* 3 (2):127-49.

Calhoun, C. 1998. Community without Propinquity Revisited: Communications Technology and the Transformation of the Urban Public Sphere. *Sociological Inquiry 68* (3):373-97.

Della Porta, D. 1999. Political Protest, Protesters, and Protest Policing: Public Discourse in Italy and Germany from the 1960s to the 1980s. In *How Social Movements Matter*, edited by M. Giugni, D. McAdam, and C. Tilly, 66-96. Minneapolis: University of Minnesota Press.

Eisinger, P. K. 1973. The Conditions of Protest Behaviour in American Cities. *American Political Science Review* 67:11-28.

Goldner, M. 2001. Expanding Political Opportunities and Changing Collective Identities in the Complementary and Alternative Medicine Movement. In *Political Opportunities, Social Movements and Democratization*, edited by P. G. Coy, 69-102. Oxford: Elsevier/JAI.

Grinberg, L. 2014. Comparing Occupy Movements: Global Mobilizing Power, Local Political Context and Dynamic. XVIII ISA World Congress, Yokohama, Japan, 13-19 July.

Hermann, T. 2009. *The Israeli Peace Movement—A Shattered Dream*. New York: Cambridge University Press.

Hermann, T. et al. 2014. *The Israeli Democracy Index 2014*. Jerusalem: The Israel Democracy Institute.

Kitschelt, H. P. 1986. Political Opportunity Structures and Political Protest: Anti-Nuclear Movements in Four Democracies. *British Journal of Political Science* 16 (1):57-86.

Koopmans, R. and D. Rucht. 2002. Protest Event Analysis. In *Methods of Social Movement Research*, edited by B. Klandermans and S. Staggenborg, 231-59. Minneapolis: University of Minnesota Press.

McCarthy, J. D. 1996. Constraints and Opportunities in Adopting, Adapting and Inventing. In *Comparative Perspectives on Social Movements: Political Opportunities, Mobilizing Structures, and Cultural Framings*, edited by D. McAdam, J. D. McCarthy and M. N. Zald, 141-51. New York: Cambridge University Press.

McCarthy, J. and M. Zald, 1977. Resource Mobilization and Social Movements: A Partial Theory. *American Journal of Sociology* 82(6):1212-41.

Melucci, A. 1995. The Process of Collective Identity. In *Social Movements and Culture*, edited by H. Johnston and B. Klandermans, 41-63. Minneapolis: University of Minnesota Press.

Meyer, D. S., and D. Minkoff. 2004. Conceptualizing Political Opportunity. *Social Forces* 82 (4):1457-92.

Rosenhek, Z. and M. Shalev. 2013. The Political Economy of Israel's "Social Justice" Protests: A Class and Generational Analysis. *Contemporary Social Science: Journal of the Academy of Social Sciences*. http://dx.doi.org/10.1080/21582041.2013.851405

Rotman, A., M. Shalev and Y. Shavit. 2014. Where Did the Protest Come From? A Spatial and Political Analysis of Israel's 2011 Social Protest. Draft paper for the Reclaiming the City Square workshop, Tel Aviv University, April.

Shecheter, A. 2012. *Rothschild—A Chronology of Protest*. Tel Aviv: Hakibbutz Hameuchad and Sifriat Poalim [Hebrew].

Suh, D. 2001. How Do Political Opportunities Matter for Social Movements: Political Opportunity, Misframing, Pseudosuccess, and Pseudofailure. *The Sociological Quarterly* 42 (3):437-60.

Snow, D. A. and R. D. Benford. 1988. Ideology, Frame Resonance and Participant Mobilization. In *From Structure to Action: Comparing Social Movement Research across Cultures*, edited by B. Klandermans, H. Kriesi, and S. Tarrow, 197-219. Greenwich, CT: JAI Press.

Tarrow, S. 1996. States and Opportunities: The Political Structuring of Social Movements. In *Comparative Perspectives on Social Movements: Political Opportunities, Mobilizing Structures, and Cultural Framings*, edited by D. McAdam, J. D. McCarthy and M. N. Zald, 41-61. New York: Cambridge University Press.

———. 2001. Silence and Voice in the Study of Contentious Politics: Introduction. In *Silence and Voice in the Study of Contentious Politics*, edited by R. Aminzade, et al., 1-13. Cambridge, UK: Cambridge University Press.

Tilly, C. 1978. *From Mobilization to Revolution*. MA: Reading: Addison-Wesley.

———. 1999. From Interactions to Outcomes in Social Movements. In *How Social Movements Matter*, edited by M. G. Giugni, D. McAdam and C. Tilly, 253-70. Minneapolis: University of Minnesota Press.

Wood, M. and M. Flinders. 2014. Rethinking Depoliticisation: Beyond the Governmental. *Policy & Politics* 42 (2):151-70.

Young, N. 1986. The Peace Movement: A Comparative and Analytical Survey. *Alternatives* 11 (2):185-217.

7. Economic Demands and Sociocultural Identities: The "Social Justice" Protests in Israel

Zeev Rosenhek and Michael Shalev

Similar to other phenomena that are understood as global, the wave of mass protests that emerged in many advanced capitalist societies during 2011-12, has exhibited a combination of common supra-national features and idiosyncratic local traits. These protest movements have a number of characteristics in common: the initiators and leaders of the protests are educated young people with middle-class backgrounds, protesting against their own reduced economic opportunities and the widening inequality between the wealthy and the rest of the population; their mobilisation expresses deep alienation from institutionalised politics; they occupy public space in an attempt to imbue it with new meanings and instil alternative forms of political action; they hold mass demonstrations attended by broader audiences; and they make diffuse demands on the state for more or less radical changes to the economy and socio-economic policies—demands that are fundamentally redistributive.[1] The movements also share similar practices of protest and collective action: the wide use of theatrical performativity; a reliance on digital technologies and new media to spread their message and mobilise activists; network logic of action and organisation; and an effort to implement direct democracy and non-hierarchical coordination.[2]

These features were shared by the protests that unexpectedly broke out in Israel in the summer of 2011 under the slogan "the people demand social justice," and succeeded in dominating the public agenda for two tumultuous months. The global wave of protests doubtless expanded the structure of political opportunities for the Israeli movement by offering models for imitation and ideational frameworks for identification and legitimation. Similarly to the Spanish, Greek and Portuguese cases, the

Israeli protest successfully garnered support from far beyond the internal nucleus of activists, mobilising mass rallies with often unprecedented numbers of supporters who had not previously participated in this kind of protest activity over economic and social issues. Yet the protests in Israel emerged in unusual circumstances. As we show below, economic conditions differed profoundly from those that struck such a blow to Western Europe and the US following the financial crisis that erupted in 2008. Furthermore, the legacy of protest politics in Israel—and politics in general—also differed from those in most established democracies. Since 1967, if not before, they have been dominated by Israel's protracted conflict with Arab states and the Palestinians, and by the future of the Occupied Territories—issues that are related to conflicts over competing definitions of collective identity in Israeli society. Distributive conflicts and issues have been marginalised and have failed to serve as a platform for mass political mobilisation.

Our aim in this paper is to analyse the connections between the socio-economic character of the protests and processes of collective identity formation that evolved around the massive mobilisation that took place in Israel during the summer of 2011. Making broad and inclusionary demands for a comprehensive welfare state and a more equal distribution of economic resources, the protest movement attempted to articulate an all-embracing Israeli collective identity intended to transcend the deep-seated and long-lasting socio-political and cultural divides characterising Israeli society. In its efforts to cross deeply entrenched sociocultural boundaries emerging from solidarities based on ethnicity, religiosity, lifestyle and cultural-political habitus, the protests indeed represented a remarkable novelty in Israeli politics. We examine the tensions between the material and cultural interests of the protest's initiators deriving from their class-generational background on the one hand and their attempt to build an inclusive identity that would rise above societal cleavages and conflicts on the other, as a key dynamics that fundamentally affected the protest's character and trajectory. Focusing on the dialectic relationship and tensions between an inclusionary formulation of membership and demands and pre-existing deep socio-political and cultural divides, the analysis contributes to the study of the character and dynamics of the presumably all-encompassing movements that comprise the current global wave of protest.

Socio-Political Divides and the Current Wave of Protests

For three decades sociologists have been raising questions about the relevance of material life chances, class identities, distributive demands and socio-economic issues in general for collective action in both institutionalised and non-institutionalised politics.[3] Scholars have highlighted the increasing importance of post-materialist sociocultural issues and conflicts as the primary bases for political mobilisation at the expense of the class identities and distributive demands that used to play such an important role in the political dynamics of capitalist societies until the final quarter of the twentieth century.[4] According to this approach, political struggles in contemporary societies are more likely to form around questions of values and lifestyle than around the unequal distribution of economic resources. The conceptualisation of post-industrial societies as founded on post-materialist identities and values is also embodied in the "new social movements" paradigm, which has dominated the study of social movements for decades.[5]

This approach sharply distinguished between the classic protest movements of advanced capitalist societies and those that emerged since the student movement of the 1960s. The distinction refers to the collective grievances and identities constructed and expressed by the movements, as well as to features of their activists and supporters and the political practices they use. The classic protest movements were strongly related to identities formed in connection to the economic arena; they expressed material concerns and interests; put forward distributive demands; were led or supported by the organised working class; and deployed highly institutionalised practices, usually linked to hierarchically organised labour unions or left-wing parties. The new social movements, by contrast, emerged tightly associated with identities that were formulated on the basis of cultural distinctions and lifestyle, and their demands were mainly related to post-materialist values and the recognition of those distinct identities.[6] Even when some of the issues dealt with by certain of these movements had a clearly distributive aspect, their demands were primarily framed in terms of the recognition of the distinct culturally-based identities of excluded and oppressed groups. Some of the more notable examples of these new social movements are the women's movements, student movements, the gay rights movement, the movements against nuclear arms and energy, and the environmental movement. The main support base of these movements is the educated middle- and upper-middle classes, especially their younger members. They are also characterised by a principled rejection of institutionalised politics and by practices that aim to underscore this rejection: fluid and seemingly non-hierarchical organisational structures; participatory democracy and deliberative decision-making; and creative and innovative protest activities in which humour and playfulness play a central part.[7]

The recent wave of protest in advanced capitalist societies—from the Portuguese Geração à Rasca ("desperate generation") and Indignados in Spain, through the Occupy Wall Street movement in the US to the social justice movement in Israel—poses a serious challenge to the dichotomous distinction between old materialistic social movements and new post-materialistic ones. On the one hand, the current wave of protest shares many characteristics with the new social movements: the instigators, leaders and many of the supporters are youngsters with a middle-class background, and they are generally university students or graduates. Moreover, following the development of these practices by the preceding anti-globalisation movement, the contemporary protests have further expanded the fluid and participatory internal practices and forms of protest characteristic of new social movements. At the same time, however, the recent protest wave took shape around opposition to existing modes of resource distribution and demands for alternative socio-economic policies. Finally, in the process of repoliticising socio-economic issues, these movements have attempted to construct new collective identities based on quasi-class distinctions. While there is no longer talk of "the working class" or "the labour movement," these new identities are nonetheless constructed and formulated in relation to the structure of social inequality: "the 99% vs. the 1%" in the US; "the people against bankers and politicians" in Spain; and "the middle class versus the tycoons" in Israel. In this regard, the current protests rearticulate the relationship between socio-political identities and distributive conflicts as the basis for political action.

A Thoroughly Unexpected Protest

The Israeli protests began in the wake of Internet campaigns by disgruntled consumers during the first half of 2011. The opening step was an encampment in the heart of the Tel Aviv financial district, inspired by the Spanish model, which was designed to draw attention to the housing problems faced by young students.[8] Enthusiastically publicised and supported by most of the mainstream media, the protest quickly expanded in three directions: establishment of parallel tent camps in other locations around the country; support by and collaboration with diverse cause groups and lobbying groups, most importantly the national union of students; and a series of half a dozen mass rallies that peaked on September 3 with an unprecedented turnout of 300,000 in Tel Aviv and 100,000 in other areas of the country. Both the demands and the collective identity adopted by the protest broadened as it developed, from an initial emphasis on housing and other consumer issues to a redefinition as a middle-class protest with aspirations to represent "the people" in a struggle for "social justice." In addition to students and young people, the protest leaders embraced other segments of society including striking medical residents and parents complaining about the cost of childcare, and made efforts to reach out to marginalised groups, primarily Jewish residents of poor neighbourhoods and the socio-geographical periphery.

In retrospect, it is tempting to see the Israeli protest as the inevitable consequence of more than two decades of radical neoliberal policies that undermined the economic and social security of large segments of the Israeli population. But at the time, the remarkable success of the movement in mobilising wide public support took all observers of Israeli society and politics utterly by surprise. It was hard to believe that 400,000 Israelis would take to the streets over issues such as the distribution of wealth in society, and social and economic policy. First, as noted, the protest in Israel emerged in entirely different economic circumstances from those prevalent in the US and much of Europe. The protests there were the result of a deep and lasting economic crisis that hit a large part of the population extremely hard, including the middle class, and particularly its younger generation. Moreover, in countries where the financial crisis was redefined as a public debt crisis, states adopted austerity policies that involved deep cutbacks in public expenditure, which seriously harmed both social rights and the employment opportunities of young adults from the middle class. Given that those states were simultaneously channelling trillions of taxpayers' dollars into failing banks and financial institutions, one of the central motifs of the protests was that massive public resources were being diverted to save the very financial capitalists and their lackeys who had caused the crisis, while as a consequence, the remainder of the population was obliged to suffer radical contraction of the welfare state.

In Israel, by contrast, on the eve of the protests the global crisis had not significantly harmed domestic economic performance. The financial market remained relatively stable, no bailouts and massive monetary injection were necessary and there was no real threat of a debt crisis. From the second half of 2009 Israel enjoyed favourable growth rates by international standards, and unemployment declined in 2010 to less than 7% (twice that among the young), one of the lowest levels experienced since 1985. Furthermore, in 2010 and 2011 no severe cutbacks to public budgets were on the agenda. Nevertheless, as we explain below, these indicators conceal a far more complex socio-economic reality characterised not only by ever-widening gaps in the distribution of economic resources, but also by relative deterioration in the economic opportunities of the younger generation as a whole, and that of the middle class in particular. Be that as it may, in the summer of 2011 Israel was exempt from either the socio-economic distress or the atmosphere of a deep crisis demanding radical change in the political economy which were the basis for the protest movements in other countries.

The Israeli protest was also surprising because of the striking contrast it posed to the cleavages and identities that had characterised the political field and contentious mobilisation in Israel since 1967. These were all primarily organised around issues of war and peace with the Palestinians and the region's Arab states, and the future of the Occupied Territories. These issues had been central in both institutionalised and non-institutionalised politics, and had largely defined the socio-political identities of different groups, voting patterns, and the demands of most of the country's protest movements. The main extra-parliamentary movements that had successfully positioned themselves at the top of the political agenda and were responsible for the largest mass mobilisations emerged around these issues, such as the opposing movements regarding the future of the Occupied Territories (Peace Now and *Gush Emunim*), and those targeted to support of or opposition to either ceding territory for peace (first with Egypt, later with the Palestinians) or controversial actions by the Israeli military.[9] Additional political conflicts that sometimes occupied the centre of the public stage—and especially the conflict between Israel's religious and secular populations—were closely related to competing views concerning war and peace issues and to the wider political question of the ethno-national definition of the Israeli state and society. Consequently, the main political conflicts in Israel were perceived and interpreted as enacting a fundamental struggle between contradictory political and cultural collective identities. While the 1970s and 1980s saw instances of protest over issues of distribution, they reached nothing like the scale of mass mobilisation seen in the protest of 2011.[10]

Given this type of politics, in which social conflicts were understood and formulated in terms of clashes between fundamental cultural identities, distributive issues and class interests played a marginal role in politics, serving as only a muted or implicit political cleavage. Even when the material interests of different groups formed the basis for their organisation and political action, they were understood and portrayed in terms of cultural identities—mainly religious and/or ethnic—or in terms of an effort at attaining peace and democratisation.[11] Although public support for the welfare state and expressions of concern about the increasing economic inequality were more pronounced in Israel than in most other developed countries,[12] until the summer of 2011 those issues did not produce large protest movements or mass political mobilisation, and they were certainly not the grounds for the construction of socio-political identities.

The third factor that should have narrowed the structure of political opportunities for the emergence of a mass social protest in Israel is related to the rise in recent decades of alienation and mistrust towards politics and politicians, often described as anti-politics.[13] It would seem that most Israelis became indifferent, antithetical even, to politics. This atmosphere of anti-politics was felt not only in declining turnouts at election time, but also in what would seem to be a reduced propensity to take part in protest activities.[14] In the context of the accelerated liberalisation of Israel's political economy and the penetration of individualistic and consumerist principles into many spheres of life, the neoliberal project of depoliticising economic policy, and indeed economics in general, and its definition as the preserve of "apolitical" experts, was remarkably successful in Israel.[15]

It appeared that most Israelis, especially among the middle class, were not at all interested in taking part in collective action with political objectives, particularly when those objectives were related to the politics of the distribution of resources. Moreover, rising apathy towards and revulsion from politics were viewed as particularly notable among the younger members of the middle class—a generation that was portrayed in public discourse as hedonistic, radically individualistic, and indifferent to matters of public import, particularly those of a socio-economic nature. However, it was precisely this class-generational unit that launched and led a protest that raised the banner of solidarity and social justice.

Class-Generational Dynamics and Israel's Protests

In class and generational terms the initiators and leaders of the 2011 protest, as well as the main circle of supporters, were the children of the liberalisation of Israel's political economy.[16] They grew up in middle- and upper-middle class families in the 1990s and the early 2000s just as most members of those classes were enjoying a significant improvement in their standard of living and were adopting modes of conspicuous consumption previously unknown in Israel. Their parents were the main beneficiaries of the liberalisation of the Israeli economy, and this shaped their experiences as a class-generational unit. However, when reaching early adulthood, they found themselves in a situation where the successful reproduction of their parents' life chances was in no way guaranteed, including the level and modes of consumption to which they had become accustomed during their formative years. The same features of the liberalised political economy that had formed the basis for their parents' significantly improved life chances since the 1990s, had become a hindrance to many of the younger generation seeking to reproduce their class position. In other words, many of the sons and daughters of the beneficiaries of the neoliberal regime became its losers.

Current aspirants to middle class life chances and lifestyle enter a labour market bereft of many of the protections that used to be afforded to workers. The labour conditions, salaries and employment security of young workers in a large swathe of the contemporary labour market—including many professionals—are far worse than they used to be, prior to processes of neoliberal "flexibilisation."[17] Irregular forms of employment through manpower agencies or subcontractors that first appeared in non-professional fields have been spreading to several professions commonly taken up by young people with higher education, particularly women and especially in the public sector. Similar to what occurred in many other countries, these processes have created a new *precariat* composed of educated young people from middle-class backgrounds.[18]

The life chances of those young adults were also undermined by welfare state reforms. While the most drastic cutbacks, mainly since 2003, were made to programmes that targeted the lower classes—such as unemployment insurance, guaranteed minimum income and child benefits—the Israeli welfare state also contracted in areas that are important to the middle class. Reduced public spending on education and health and the heavy cost of childcare and quasi-private education for young children hurt young middle-class families, who today have to pay for services that their parents were given for free, or at least were heavily subsidised. The drastic reduction in state support for the middle class in the realm of housing is particularly notable. During the 1990s, mortgage schemes for young couples that included a significant state subsidy that primarily benefited the middle class were almost entirely eliminated. In parallel, the difficulty of buying a home increased as a result of large price rises in real terms. Those who managed to buy a property had to make far higher mortgage repayments than their parents had in the 1970s when they bought their first apartment with substantial governmental subsidies.

The generational dynamics of the economic situation of the Israeli middle class explains the unease which was at the root of the unexpected emergence of a mass protest movement around distributive issues and material interests. The children of Israel's liberalisation found themselves in a situation where capitalism's promise of inter-generational improving standard of living failed to be met. In light of what appears to be a failure in the inter-generational reproduction of the life chances of a sizable segment of the middle class, this class-generational unit sought to position itself at the forefront of a broad movement issuing wide-ranging distributive demands in the name of "the people." As we shall see in the following section, the protest movement embodied an effort to rearticulate material interests and demands while coping with divisions and conflicts formulated in terms of cultural identities—that is, to manoeuvre between a politics of redistribution and a politics of recognition.

Inclusionary Demands and Socio-Political Identities

As we have noted, the mass mobilisation that emerged around distributive issues in 2011 represented to a large extent a novel mode of political action in Israel. However, this is not to say that it was detached from the principles that have organised the political field in Israel for the past four decades: socio-political identities based on cultural distinctions and conflicts over non-economic issues. The complex relationship between the protest and pre-existing identities and conflicts in Israeli society was central to the public debate that emerged around it: the conflict between left and right (as they are defined in Israel), between the secular and the ultra-Orthodox, between the Ashkenazi (European origin) centre and the Mizrahi (Middle Eastern origin) periphery, between rich and spoiled Tel Aviv and the rest of the country—

all these conflicts and their associated identities were both simultaneously present in and absent from the protest and the discourse surrounding it.

At the most overt level, the protest made broad and inclusive demands on the state. Alongside the demand to improve the life chances of the middle class, and especially its younger generation, demands were also made for expanding state aid and social protection to the disadvantaged. The combination of a wide range of specific demands with the all-inclusive demand for social justice and solidarity and the attribution of responsibility to the state for its citizens' welfare, created the impression that the protest movement was actually demanding the rebuilding of a universal welfare state that would advance a more egalitarian distribution of resources. The leaders of the protest movement apparently hoped that these demands would serve as basis for the construction of a "pan-Israeli" socio-political identity that would rise above the old familiar political and cultural identities and conflicts, especially those related to the future of the Occupied Territories and secular-religious relations. The aim was to create an inclusive identity representing the general social interest, which would transcend the old divisions and quarrels—in the face of corrupt politicians, of governments, past and present, which abrogated responsibility for their citizens, and "tycoons" who were exploiting the people. This inclusionary formulation of membership in the collective was a key theme recurring in almost all statements by the leaders and activists of the protests.[19]

To be sure, in terms of public support and participation in mass demonstrations, the protest was remarkably successful in crossing entrenched social and cultural boundaries. While launched by young, educated, left-wing and secular Tel Avivians, the protest was embraced by diverse segments of the population whom the former tried to construct as "the Israelis." For example, according to a survey carried out a few weeks after the protests began, 88% of all respondents said they were either very or quite supportive.[20] In this regard, the Israeli protests were similar to the preceding 15M movement in Spain, where tent encampments in the main squares sparked mass demonstrations throughout the country with participants and supporters who were far more diverse in terms of both generation and class than the inner circle of activists.

However, if we look below the surface, it turns out that the protest remained strongly bound to the same identities and conflicts that have structured politics in Israel since the 1970s. Public support varied significantly between different sections of the Jewish population, mirroring the classic divisions of Israeli society and politics. Left-leaning Israelis supported and participated in the protest more than those on the right; the secular more than the religious; the educated more than the less educated; and middle to high-earners more than low-earners.[21] These differences in support and participation reflect the tension between the effort to construct the protest as expressing the interests of all Israelis, and its class-related socio-political foundations. The core of the protest remained largely the domain of the Ashkenazi, secular, educated and "left wing" middle class. Furthermore, competition and conflicts between different groups among the protesters based on class and ethnic divisions soon emerged, reflecting diverse, and sometimes opposed, identities, grievances and claims.[22]

The tension between inclusiveness and privilege was also expressed in the republican motifs mobilised in the protests, which have always been a central basis for claims-making by the privileged in Israeli politics.[23] The protesters' demands were often justified in relation to the contribution of the middle class to society, in terms of both military service and its contribution to the economy. In this way, protest leaders sought to constitute a collective socio-political identity which represented the middle class as a "universal class," expressing, serving and advancing the common good. The centrality of this motif was clearly manifested in the results of the 2013 elections, particularly in the remarkable success of the newly established party "There is a future" (*Yesh Atid*), which won 19 seats in the Parliament (out of 120) and became the second largest party after the Likud. Established and led by Yair Lapid, a TV celebrity-turned-politician who was appointed Minister of Finance after the elections, the party capitalised on the protests and built its electoral campaign on the grievances and claims of the secular middle class. It presented itself as the true and only representative of this "universal class"—defined as those who contribute to the country by working, paying taxes and serving in the military but are neglected by the state, as opposed to those who get benefits without contributing, especially the Ultra-Orthodox population.

In more general terms, the call for social justice can be interpreted as an attempt by the middle class to reposition itself at the centre of the political and social fields as the backbone of society. During the 1990s, the middle class in Israel had attempted to construct itself as the universal class that promoted the common good through the peace project. However, after the collapse of the Oslo process and in a political context in which a discourse based on peace-making was no longer accepted as representing the common good, but rather the opposite, the middle class turned instead to distributive issues and social justice, not only in order to improve its life chances but also in order to regain recognition and socio-political dominance. This aspiration was reinforced by the persistent political dominance of a coalition of the nationalist right wing and ultra-orthodox parties. Members of the secular middle class felt that they had been pushed to the margins by these dominant forces, which were orchestrating a full-frontal assault on the values and practices of liberal democracy. In response, the protest movement was also a way to rebuild the collective identity of the secular and "left wing" middle class. Mass demonstrations were an opportunity for this group to take to the streets and celebrate solidarity, after a long absence from the public sphere as a collective. The protest thus not only embodied a politics of distribution, which formed its overt outer layer, but also an implicit inner layer driven by a politics of status and recognition managed by a social sector that sought to reclaim its dominance through a revised collective identity.

What emerges, therefore, is an interesting reversal in the relationship between material interests and sociocultural identities. Israeli politics has long blurred material interests and class categories as bases for political action, and demands on the state have been couched in terms of the recognition of distinct sociocultural identities. The protest of 2011 re-articulated the relations between these two dimensions. Its demands were explicitly formulated in distributive terms as opposition to economic inequality and to the state's withdrawal from responsibility for the welfare of its citizens. The protesters and their supporters portrayed their action as a new inclusionary politics that would replace the old, Balkanised struggles between culturally-defined "sectors." However, while the protest was undoubtedly innovative in comparison to traditional Israeli politics, this does not imply that the old socio-political divides simply vanished; rather, they changed their location. The group which had insistently disowned the strategy of political mobilisation on the basis of an explicit "sectoral" identity, implicitly did precisely that in the backstage of the protests.

Conclusions

Israel's "social justice" movement was even more encompassing than the mass protests that preceded it in Spain, Portugal and Greece. Yet it was an improbable candidate for such inclusivity, given that the Israeli movement had to contend with deeply-institutionalised socio-political cleavages and lacked the unifying and motivating stimulus of radical state-imposed austerity. We have argued that the material foundation of the Israeli protest resulted from a generational shift in the life chances of the middle class, shaped by Israel's transition to a neoliberal political-economic regime. The institutionalisation of the neoliberal model in Israel in the early 2000s undermined the promise of inter-generational reproduction of middle class life chances for significant numbers of the younger generation of that class.

However, alongside this class-generational dynamic, the protest was also closely linked to pre-existing social and cultural identities and the conflicts between them. In this sense, the subtext of the protest can be interpreted as a bid by the secular and "left wing" middle class to reclaim its social dominance by reinventing itself as a universal class under the flag of inclusiveness and social justice. The tension between the material and cultural interests of the protest's instigators and their attempt to build an inclusive identity that would rise above societal cleavages and conflicts percolated through many aspects of the protest. In this regard, it remained deeply embedded in the distinguishing features of the Israeli political field for the last forty years.

We opened this paper by referring to other protest movements that emerged in advanced capitalist countries following the deep economic crisis that started in 2007, but with only cursory reference to the causal role of this protest wave for the Israeli case. Occupy-type protests in western countries and preceding popular uprisings in some Arab states certainly played a part in the Israeli protest, despite sharp differences in political and economic circumstances. Similar to other global phenomena, there were processes of diffusion through which ideas and practices crossed national boundaries, often based on concrete networks of relationships between activists from different countries. Furthermore, the global wave of protests expanded the structure of political opportunities for the protest in Israel by providing models for imitation and ideational frameworks for identification and legitimation. And yet, the specific traits of the Israeli political field, particularly the deep-seated sociocultural divides that characterise it, played the key role in shaping the form and trajectory of the protests in Israel.

Notes

1. Benjamin Tejerina and Ignacia Perugorria, *From Social to Political: New Forms of Mobilization and Democratization, Conference Proceedings* (Bilbao: Universidad del Pais Vasco, 2012).
2. W. Lance Bennett and Alexandra Segerberg, "The Logic of Connective Action," in *Information, Communication & Society* 2012, no. 15 (5):739-68; Manuel Castells, *Networks of outrage and hope: Social movements in the Internet Age* (Cambridge UK: Polity, 2012); Paul Mason, *Why it's kicking off everywhere: The new global revolutions* (London: Verso, 2012).
3. Terry Nichols Clark and Seymour Martin Lipset, *The Breakdown of Class Politics: A Debate on Post-Industrial Stratification* (Baltimore: Johns Hopkins University Press, 2001); , Geoffrey Evans, *The End of Class Politics? Class Voting in Comparative Context* (Oxford: Oxford University Press, 1999).
4. Herbert Kitschelt, *The Transformation of European Social Democracy* (Cambridge UK: Cambridge University Press, 1994).
5. Ronald Inglehart, *Cultural Shift in Advanced Industrial Society* (Princeton: Princeton University Press, 1990); Enrique Larana, Hank Johnston and Joseph R. Gusfield, *New social movements: From ideology to identity* (Philadelphia: Temple University Press, 1994).
6. Hanspeter Kriesi, Ruud Koopmans, Jan Willem Duyvendak and Marco G. Giugni, *New social movements in Western Europe: a comparative analysis* (Minneapolis: University of Minnesota Press, 1995); George Steinmetz, "Regulation theory, post-Marxism, and the new social movements," in *Comparative Studies In Society and History*, no. 36 (1):176-212, 1994.
7. Enrique Larana, Hank Johnston and Joseph R. Gusfield, *New social movements: From ideology to identity* Philadelphia: Temple University Press, 1994).
8. Eitan Y. Alimi, "'Occupy Israel': A Tale of Startling Success and Hopeful Failure." *Social Movement Studies* 2012, no. 11 (3-4):402-7; Lev Luis Grinberg," The J14 resistance mo(ve)ment: The Israeli Mix of Tahrir and Puerta Del Sol," in *Current Sociology* 2013, no. 61 (4):491-509.
9. Tamar Hermann, *The Israeli Peace Movement: A Shattered Dream* (Cambridge: Cambridge University Press, 2009).
10. Sam N. Lehman-Wilzig, *Stiff-necked people, bottle-necked system: the evolution and roots of Israeli public protest, 1949-1986* (Bloomington: Indiana University Press, 1990).
11. Dani Filc, *Populism and Hegemony in Israel* (Tel-Aviv: Resling Publishing [in Hebrew], 2006); Yoav Peled, "Towards a Redefinition of Jewish Nationalism in Israel? The Enigma of Shas," in *Ethnic and Racial Studies* 1998, no. 21 (4):703-27; Michael Shalev and Gal Levy, "The Winners and Losers of 2003: Ideology, Social Structure and Political Change," in Asher Arian and Michal Shamir (eds.), *The Elections in Israel—2003* (Brunswick NJ: Transaction Books, 2005), pp. 212-32.
12. Michael Shalev, "The Welfare State Consensus in Israel: Placing Class Politics in Context," in Steffen Mau and Benjamin Veghte (eds.), *Social Justice, Legitimacy and the Welfare State* (Aldershot: Ashgate Publishing Ltd., 2007).
13. Asher Arian and Michal Shamir, "On mistaking a dominant party in a dealigning system," in Asher Arian and Michal Shamir (eds.), *The elections in Israel, 2003* (New Brunswick: Transaction Publishers, 2005), pp. 13-31. Dani Filc, "Neo-Liberalism, Sovereignty, and the Crisis of Representation in Israel," in Tamar Hermann (ed.), *By the People, For the*

People, Without the People? The Emergence of (Anti)Political Sentiment in Western Democracies and in Israel (Jerusalem: The Israel Democracy Institute, 2012), pp. 226-46.

14. Yael Yishai, "Escape from Politics: The Case of Israel," in Tamar Hermann (ed.), *By the People, For the People, Without the People? The Emergence of (Anti)Political Sentiment in Western Democracies and in Israel* (Jerusalem: The Israel Democracy Institute, 2012), pp. 288-313.
15. Daniel Maman and Zeev Rosenhek, *The Israeli Central Bank: Political Economy, Global Logics and Local Actors* (London: Routledge, 2011).
16. We elaborate on the class-generational sources of the protests in Zeev Rosenhek and Michael Shalev, "The Political Economy of Israel's 'Social Justice' Protests: A Class and Generational Analysis," in *Contemporary Social Science* 2014, no. 9 (1):31-48.
17. Amir Paz-Fuchs, "Objectionable Work in Israel," in *Comparative Labour Law and Policy Journal* 2009, no. 31:471-86.
18. Guy Standing, *The Precariat—The New Dangerous Class* (London: Bloomsbury Academic, 2011).
19. Asher Schechter, *Rothschild: The Story of a Protest Movement* (Tel Aviv: Hakibbutz Hameuchad Publishing House [in Hebrew], 2012).
20. Tamar Hermann, *The Israeli Democracy Index, 2011* (Jerusalem: The Israel Democracy Institute, 2011).
21. Tamar Hermann, ibid.
22. Asher Schechter, ibid.; Yossi Yonah, *Cracks in the Wall: The Israeli Social Protest of 2011* (Jerusalem: Keter [in Hebrew], 2015).
23. Gershon Shafir and Yoav Peled, *Being Israeli—The Dynamics of Multiple Citizenship* (Cambridge: Cambridge University Press, 2002).

Movements and Counter-Movements

8. Amid Empire States: Protest Movements in the Transforming Middle East

Fatemeh Sadeghi

Introduction

The political uprisings of the North African and Middle Eastern countries have been novel and unthinkable in various ways. The novelty, however, is not restricted merely to the conditions or the repertoire for action, including slogans, collectivity, organisations, new media and social networks and street protests. The unexpected consequences of the majority of these movements include also their failure to challenge the political structure. Some of these movements have succeeded to overthrow the authoritarian regimes, while others have been brutally suppressed. Some of them have been deformed and backlashed, while others have burst into civil war, internal conflicts and fragmentation. Although Middle Eastern protest movements have been investigated from different perspectives, broader conditions such as state and society structures, internal, regional and international power relations are not sufficiently taken into consideration. In fact they have been either underestimated or ignored. This is while they seem to have deeply influenced the fate of these movements. Therefore, the eruption, procedure and the fate of these movements require to be explained by alternative frameworks in which these relations are taken into account. Exploring internal, regional and international aspects of these movements, this paper tries to put them within a broader context of socio-economic, political and existential developments that took place in the Middle Eastern societies in recent decades. This framework may help understand the nature of these movements as well as some reasons for their failure.

In recent years, Middle Eastern states have experienced a structural transformation, from nation state to the state of emergency. Although the nation states of this region have hardly been accountable, they were concerned with legitimacy and popularity. On the contrary, emergency states tend to circumvent legitimacy. Parallel to the global trend, capital accumulation and over-accumulation allow emergency states to rule by other means such as crony capitalism. This enabled them also to curtail, crush and deform oppositional protest movements.

It seems that considering the over-accumulation of the three main states of the region, namely, Turkey, Iran and Saudi Arabia, they had been moving towards being empire states, requiring more space and territory and broader involvement in regional affairs. This transformation seems to have deep impacts on protest movements of the Middle East, namely, the Green Movement in Iran, the Gezi movement in Turkey, the Syrian uprising, the Human Rights Movement of Bahrain, and revolutionary movements in Egypt, Tunisia, and Libya. All of these movements have been either crushed or deformed. In either case, they failed to bring about desired results. Except for government's suppressions, this failure is partly rooted in fragmented and provisional mobilisation of these movements suffering from internal fractions across class, religion, ethnicity and tribe.

By and large, these revolutions and movements seem very much similar to the 1848 revolutions that broke out in different parts of Europe but in the end burst into failure and brought about a wave of depression and disillusionment among many revolutionaries.

From Nation States to the States of Emergency

State-society relations have dramatically changed in the Middle East over the past decades. In different parts of the region, ordinary life of millions of people has dramatically deteriorated compared to the past. Different aspects of life including society, economy, politics and environment seem to be in a critical situation. The states seem to be a part and parcel of this situation, if not its creator. Structural developments of the state and society signal a new era, whose features diverge from the age of nation states of the early and mid-twentieth century. Previous nation states seem to have been gradually replaced by emergency states whose function and aims are different from those of nation states. Rather than governing societies, they tend to be sovereign through policing apparatus, neoliberal and crony capitalist relations and hegemonic expansion in space and time. Therefore, unlike the nationalist era, when the states aimed at constructing distinctive national units on the basis of definite borders and territories, unified language, religion and homogeneous race, the emergency states have other ambitions.

The state of emergency is divergent from nation state politically, socially, economically and even existentially.

The state of emergency is not a new phenomenon, but it has never been as hegemonic as it is today. However, the term "state" goes far beyond governmental apparatus. It also includes position, condition, status, stature and station. The Arabic Synonym for state is *vaz*', which means also status, condition, position and situation. In both Arabic and English it also implies place, order, arrangement and condition. A government apparatus is an emergency state when it tends to increasingly become an absolute sovereignty to which society becomes an object of manipulation and an appendix rather than raison d'être. A condition is emergency when it requires immediate and extraordinary attention. From emergency condition, something novel is expected to emerge. Therefore, "state" includes not only governmental apparatus, but also legal, economic, social and political conditions and relations, both internally and internationally. Nevertheless, the "state" and the "emergency" seem contradictory, since state in both meanings of the term implies stability, continuity and durability, whereas emergency implies instability, discontinuity and disruption. However, the state of emergency is in fact a contradictory situation, in which emergency and durability, and situatedness and instability, go hand in hand. It is an extraordinary situation, it tends to be situated and endures. It tends to be solidified as ordinary and evident, namely as non-emergent. Emergency state and state of emergency reflect and reinforce each other. The Arabic and Persian synonyms for the state of emergency are *al-vaz' al- ezterāri* and *vaz'yiat e ezterāri,* in which *ezterār* from the root of *zarr* and *zarar* means harm. *Ezterār* has also other meanings. It implies also coercion, intimidation, desperation, tangle, predicament, embarrassment and difficulty. *Al-vaz' al- ezterāri* indicated to all these intertwined implications. The state of emergency takes the legitimacy from this very situation. It justifies itself by being the only choice, to which no other alternative is imaginable. But this justification is possible only by sidelining other alternatives.

Legally, the state of emergency is used for the condition when the government is accorded an uncontested absolute authority to declare emergency situation by a military coup, shutting down newspapers, illegal arrest, torture and execution of unlimited numbers of people. Investigating the state of emergencies in the Middle East and North Africa, Andrej Zwitter concludes, "states of emergency were often put in place to stabilise a political leadership that had lost (or never had) popular legitimacy, preventively deter protests and unrests by threatening martial-law sanctions, crack down on unwanted opposition and defenders of human rights and circumvent human rights obligations that would otherwise limit administrative detention and other powers of security and military forces."[1] Yet, the fundamental question that remains to be answered is whether loss of legitimacy is the consequence of the state of emergency or whether it creates the state of emergency.

The state of emergency has been legitimated by almost all Constitutions of the Middle Eastern countries including Israel. For instance, the state of emergency, *vaz'yiat e ezterāri* has been mentioned in the article of 79 of the 1979 Iranian Constitution, whose exercise is incumbent upon the president, though he cannot exercise it more than thirty days. Nevertheless, this article contradicts the article 110 of the Constitution conceding the declaration of war and peace as a state of emergency to the Supreme Leader. Hence, the Supreme Leader is authorised by de jure and de facto authority to declare the state of emergency. Therefore, although the government has never officially declared the state of emergency, it has been exercised on various occasions. Since the rise of neo-conservatives in 2005 Iran has entered a de facto state of emergency that dramatically intensified since the eruption of the Green Movement in 2009.

Since 1967 Egypt has been legally in constant state of emergency that intensified in recent years particularly since 2013. The state of emergency has been legalised in the 1958 Constitution of Egypt, as well as the 2007, 2012 and 2014 Constitutions, although under restricted conditions. Article 148 of the 2007 Egyptian Constitution, and the article of 148 of the 2012 Constitution, legitimised the state of emergency by according unfettered power to the president, who can suspend normal conditions according to his discretion.[2]

So far as the society is concerned, tribal, ethnic, class-based and religious factionalism characterise the state of emergency, overshadowing larger inclusive solidarities. Therefore with the transformation of governing apparatuses, the society experiences dramatic changes. In the state of emergency what was ordinary becomes extraordinary. Thousands of illegal migrants seeking shelter and food, millions of dislocated people and asylum seekers, who lost their homes, jobs and beloved ones, drone wars, massive displacements, torture, execution, killings and environmental crises, are the most salient signs of the state of emergency. In the state of emergency life itself becomes extraordinary.

With the encroachment of emergency states over the past decades, relative homogeneous societies of the Middle East have been replaced by fragmented communities, each of them pursuing communal interests. Whereas in the nationalist era socio-political movements were framed around inclusive causes such as justice, freedom and equality, in the state of emergency comprehensive democratic movements become fragmented across tribal, religious, class and ethnic fractions as soon as being framed. As Hesham Salam noted on Egypt's revolution, "the fairytale narrative of a pure, democratic revolutionary struggle that can do no harm is no longer viable and has failed to capture the complexities and messiness of the social conflicts in which the January 25 Revolution was anchored. Within the multidimensional struggles that January 25 signifies, not all good things go together, as reflected in the apparent tensions we have observed between what is popularly viewed as revolutionary and what is deemed democratic … The popular mobilisation that overthrew Hosni Mubarak entailed a complex movement that included multiple long-standing struggles, in which democratisation was *only one dimension.* These struggles also encompassed a host of other ambitions such as demands for social and economic rights, distributive justice and state institutional reforms that far surpass what liberal democracy alone can offer. These struggles did not articulate in concert. On the contrary, they have often clashed over the course of the past three years, just as they did during the lead up to June 30, 2013."[3]

This seems to be the trend of other protest movements of the region, which suffer from similar divisions and factionalism. The Syrian uprising soon became fragmented across religious and ethnic factions. Yemen's Arab Spring and Libya's revolution burst into civil war. Apart from brutal suppression by the states, the protest movements of the region suffered from internal fractions that seem to be the legacy of the state of emergency.

The state of emergency also deeply influenced economic and social relations. Compared to the nation states, the governing apparatus of state of emergency is no more accountable and responding to the economic demands of its citizen. In harmony with global trends, in recent decades the previous legal regime of property was replaced by a new one across the whole region. As a result, national assets became privatised and monopolised and various aspects of life including environment, education and health care have been increasingly commodified. These developments profoundly affected the familiar ways of life, deepened socio-economic inequalities and caused environmental crisis. Whereas providing job opportunities, employment and other opportunities for various strata of the nation were hypothetically incumbent upon the nation states, the states of emergency do not hold themselves responsible for social questions. Cronyism, nepotism and increasing level of corruption are common features of the contemporary societies of the region.

In Iran, structural developments of the post-war era coincided with Rafsanjani's presidency (1989-97) and have paved the way for the encroachment of the emergency state. The trend has accelerated during Ahmadinejad's presidency (2005-13), when Iran has moved towards being an empire state thanks to the miraculous capital over-accumulation. Transformation of property law that started since the post-war era paved the way for widespread use of legal and illegal force to monopolise the economy, space, environment and territories.

In Syria, the Assad family and cronies have owned 85% of the Syrian oil revenues in 2005. Inflation, while fluctuating, has increased in relative terms almost every year since 2000, Bashar's first year in power. It reached double digits in both 2006 and 2008. The unemployment rate has also increased dramatically. While the government acknowledged a rate of around 8 per cent in 2007, the International Labour Organisation estimated the reality was more than double that. The IMF assessed Syrian unemployment at the end of December 2009 at close to 11 per cent. In June 2005, the United Nations Development Programme found that 30 per cent of Syrians (more than five million) lived in poverty, with 11 per cent (almost two million) in extreme poverty.[4] Policing state, increasing level of intimidation and sponsored corruption, have curbed the Syrian state's inclusive function even before the uprisings erupted.[5] In 2008, Transparency International ranked Syria as the second most corrupted economy in the Middle East and North Africa, after Iraq.

In Egypt, contrary to the Constitution of 1964, the military benefits from control of a large part of the economy since the introduction of the neoliberalist policies (*infitah*) by Anwar Sadat in 1970. In 1977, Mubarak had realised that the subsidies were a drain on the national budget and tried to remove them. "Between 1991 and 2009, 382 state companies were sold by Mubarak administration to private investors for a total of 9.4 billion dollars

... In spite of the impressive improvement, the overall unemployment rate remained above 9 per cent and 25 per cent for the youth that comprise a majority of the Egyptian population."[6] This is while the military owns 92 per cent of the country's lands. Thus, people have little opportunities to get access to farming lands. In such context, the charity activities of the Muslim Brotherhood were successful particularly in *ashwaiyyat* as ruralising areas of the urban settlements that have been growing as a consequence of deteriorating economic conditions of the Egyptian farmers,[7] who had no alternative other than leaving their villages. Yet, the Muslim Brotherhood also advocated the privatisation of state-owned industries soon after they seized power. Mohammad Mursi, the abducted president from the Muslim Brotherhood, has followed the same trend of the previous years.[8] All these instances manifest a similar trend: The increasing inclination of the state to become a non-state on the one hand, and the increasing inclination of the society to become a non-society on the other hand.

Various parts of the region witnessed similar developments. However, their acceleration and outcomes have been diverse. In Iran, for instance, deterioration of economic conditions, notorious embezzlements of the eight years of hardline rule, especially after the Green Movement, and the inevitable effects of international sanctions have forced the government to slow down the process. The presidential elections of 2013, in which Hasan Rohani won the competition was a direct consequence of that development. Yet, as will be explored below, this did not necessarily lead to reconsideration.

By and large, state and society relationships are much more complex in the state of emergency compared with nation states. The state of emergency goes far beyond political, legal, economic and social relations. Rather, it is an existential situation that targeted life.

Over-Accumulation: Rising of the Empire States

Although the state of emergency has swept across the whole region in recent decades, other transformation differentiates some emergency states of the region from others pushing them towards empire states. This transformation was caused and is caused by miraculous over-accumulation that took place in recent decades, which directly impacted on the protest movements of the region and beyond.

Over-accumulation is associated with internal and external territorial expansion in time and space as the main characteristic of the empires.[9]

Expansion and alliance are made to accommodate flows of capital in order to secure the heartland, accumulation of power, economic resources and political influence. As David Harvey suggests, "structured coherence usually extends well beyond pure economic exchanges, fundamental though these may be, for it typically encompasses attitudes, cultural values, beliefs and even religious and political affiliations among those capitalists and whom they employ … The necessity to produce and maintain collective goods requires that some system of governance be brought into existence and preferably formalised into systems of administration within the region. Dominant classes and hegemonic class alliances can form within the region and lend a specific character to political as well as to economic activity. They have to be concerned about public goods, and may therefore find themselves forced to engage in public activity. They find themselves forced to engage in public provision. The formation of physical and social infrastructures both to support economic activity but also to secure and promulgate cultural and educational values and many other aspects of civic life typically reinforces the coherence of what begins to emerge as a regional entity within the global economy."[10]

Before exploring the impact of this transformation on the protest movements, I will compare the accumulation rate of four countries of the region via GDP indicator. These countries include Turkey, Saudi Arabia, Iran and Egypt. The comparison is to highlight not only the reality of the state of emergency, but also the differences that exist among them. It also helps understand the situation in which the movements have erupted and the conditions that led to their failure.

Table 8.1: GDPs of Turkey, Saudi Arabia, Iran and Egypt since 2009 (billion US$)

	2009	2010	2011	2012	2013
Turkey	822.1	731.1	774.8	788.8	822.1
Saudi Arabia	429.1	526.8	669.5	734	748.4
Iran	362.7	422.6	528.4	502.7	368.9
Egypt	188.9	271.9	246	262.8	218.8

Source: World Bank

Table 8.2: GDPs of Turkey, Saudi Arabia, Iran and Egypt since 1970 (billion US$)

	1970	1980	1990	2000	2010
Turkey	17.087	68.7893	150.6763	266.5675	731.1681
Saudi Arabia	5.0144	164.3083	116.7781	188.4419	526.8115
Iran	10.5881	90.0412	116.035	101.2865	422.568
Egypt	5.0144	22.9125	43.1304	99.8385	271.9728

Source: World Bank

According to these tables, Turkey, Saudi Arabia, Iran and Egypt experienced a dramatic increase of income in recent years. In case of Turkey, Saudi and Iran this has led to an over-accumulation allowing them to expand and deepen their territorial influence extensively compared to the past.

The tables also show the obvious difference of accumulation rate among the four countries of the region, particularly between Egypt and the rest. It is noteworthy that Iran's accumulation rate has dropped since 2013 mostly due to the international economic sanctions, whereas in Turkey and Saudi Arabia the accelerating trend has continued after a provisional drop in 2009 seemingly as an impact of the global economic crisis.

Over-accumulation directly influenced the internal and external politics of these states making them expand beyond their previous territories. Saudis' engagement in Yemen and Bahrain, Iran's intervention in Iraq and Syria, and Turkey's involvement in Syria with its unprecedented anti-Israeli policy are salient instances of such inclination. Simultaneously, however, in all these countries including Egypt socio-political and economic dissatisfaction has tremendously increased compared with the past. The consequence was several uprisings across the region, but also violent oppositional responses such as the ISIL which emerged at the influence territory of Iraq and Syria as a much contested territory.

In three of these countries, meaning Iran, Egypt and Turkey protest movements erupted as a result of structural transformation whose effects on ordinary life were sensed by various strata of society. Arbitrary rule, increasing unemployment which particularly targets youth, unprecedented corruption, and inflation and environmental disasters are phenomenal in all of the societies of the region.

Below, I will briefly explain how this situation became steadily hegemonic in Iran. Yet, such process is by no means exclusive to this country. Similar trends seem to have been working in Saudi Arabia and Turkey pushing them to play the role of empire states.

Since the end of Iran-Iraq war in 1989, the IRGC (*sepāh pāsdārān*) had undertaken several construction projects paving the way for deep involvement of the military and paramilitary organisations in internal and external affairs. Yet, the full-fledged involvement of the IRGC in economic, hence, political activities was provided in the first round of Ahmadinejad's presidency. Notable among these projects was the expansion of nuclear proliferation. The process accommodated accumulation of capital accelerated by unprecedented increase in oil revenues. As a result, whereas Iran's GDP was worth US$ 192.0149 billion in 2005, it reached US$ 355.9884 billion in 2008. However, such miraculous accumulation was made mostly by dispossession. In an extraordinary effort, the hardliners have monopolised the state-owned properties and enterprises almost overnight. In 2007, the hardliners conceded these public assets to some selected cronies, particularly the IRGC, the police and the Basij (paramilitary organisation). This was an attempt to "apply" the policies of the article 144 of the Constitution of the Islamic Republic of Iran. Consequently, public urban lands, postal service, airlines, shipping, telecommunications, power generation, foreign trade, oil, banking, insurance and railways became monopolised. The IRGC and the Basij took the lion's share of the state-owned assets. In parallel to that, different private banks, many of which are directly linked to military organisations, have been established ever since. According to some estimates, about 821 Financial Credit Institutions and private banks have been registered since the declaration of this policy in 2007. Yet, these efforts were not an application of the Constitution as they were claimed to be, since article144 unequivocally declares state-owned properties as national assets, while obliging the government to keep them so.

As part of the plan, Ahmadinejad has annulled the PBO (the Plan and Budgetary Organisation) in his first round (2005-13). The function of this institution was to supervise and curtail monopolisation. The initiative was undertaken to legally protect the endeavours of the loyal segments of the regime and expand their control over the most profitable and valuable economic activities.

The new privileges were given to selected segments and organisations whereas they have already benefited from various tax-free economic activities of the so called *bonyads* (revolutionary foundations) that are exempted from accountability. Unprecedented in post-revolutionary Iran, these attempts were "to establish monopolies at the centre of power, hence dramatically change the balance of political power in favour of chosen segments against democratic demands."[11] This was clearly an act of choosing manifestation of a new orientation of the Iranian government to solidify the state's apparatus by means of constructing a new regime class.

Furthermore, crony capitalism has put some industries like communications under the direct control of security institutions. This paved the way for widespread surveillance of oppositional political activities. The significance of such efforts was clearly demonstrated in the presidential elections of 2009, when oppositional mobilisation was curtailed by means of blocking media, mobile phones, telephones, Internet and other means of communication.

In the same period, the government encouraged population growth whose rate had dramatically decreased since the post-war era reaching 1.3% in 2010. Given the high rate of unemployment, the nationalist policies seem unreasonable. Nevertheless, they become more reasonable considering the ambitious plan of the regime to be the Shiite empire state of the region. Over-accumulation accompanied by nationalist policies provided a great opportunity for the government to solidify itself and get more involved in regional and global affairs.

Similar trends are traceable in other countries of the region. Almost simultaneously unprecedented over-accumulation by dispossession took place in Saudi Arabia and Turkey pushing them towards playing a hegemonic role internally, regionally and internationally. This in turn has caused numerous competitions among these empire states over space, time and territory. Accumulation necessitates expansion in time and place differentiating the behaviour of the states from their previous situation.

Internal and external expansion of the Saudis in space and time is exemplified, among other aspects, by the state's huge construction projects. Reportedly over 98% of the Kingdom's historical and religious sites have been destroyed since 1985, according to the UK-based Islamic Heritage Research Foundation[12] and 95% of Mecca's millennium-old buildings have been demolished in the past two decades alone. Dozens of key historical sites dating back to the birth of Islam have already been wiped out and there is a scramble among archaeologists and academics to try and encourage the authorities to preserve what little remains.[13] Also, some 95 properties and 126 mosques are being demolished in Saudi Arabia to expand the Prophet's Mosque in Medina and to construct gigantic shopping malls.[14] These attempts are associated with construction of new cities inside the Saudi territories. Also, in 2014 Saudi Arabia has become the world's biggest importer of weapons and defence equipment, which is also a significant mark of power extension.[15]

The expansion of the Saudi empire state justifies not only the suppression of the Shiite and other religious minorities inside and outside of its territories, but also the removal of the history of the sacred places from early days up to the Ottoman Empire. Accordingly, the history of the Saudis replaces the history of the Arabian Peninsula while representing itself as the history of Islam. This is expansion and accumulation in time and space.[16]

Turkey as an empire state expands in time and space not only by elimination but also by the revival of history. Neo-Ottomanism of the AK party in sheer opposition to the Saudi inclination is not nostalgia. Revival of the past actually promotes the present and the future. It legitimises greater involvement of modern Turkey in the regions that were formerly ruled by the Ottoman Empire. Taking distance from the Kemalist nation-statism, the AK party pushed Turkey towards playing an imperial role thanks to over-accumulation of this country in recent decades. Simultaneously, the legal regime of property is gradually changing through accumulation by dispossession. This is being done by means of various projects and policies to transform urban environment. For instance TOKI (Housing Development Administration of Turkey) as a main constructing agent since 2004 possessed state-owned and public properties and lands to build new houses, shopping malls, commercial compounds and speculative environments.[17]

Typology of the Middle Eastern Movements

Over-accumulation has influenced not only the ordinary life of the people of these countries, but also other societies of the region. After Saddam Hussein's fall in 2003, Iraq became an influence territory of the US imperialist expansion. With America's withdrawal from Iraq in 2011, this country has become a medium territory for the competing empire states of Turkey, Iran and Saudi Arabia. Syria has been an influence territory of both Iran and

Russia, but it became a contested medium territory of the empire states of the region since 2011. Whereas inside the empire states and their territories there may exist some space for the establishment of protest movements, in medium territories such as Iraq and later Syria, constant competition of the rival states hardly leaves any room for protest movements except for extreme violent movements such as the ISIL.

So far as the two above-mentioned related developments are concerned, i.e., the state of emergency and the empire states, the protests movements of the region can be divided into three main categories: those inside empire states, those inside influence territories and finally those outside empire states, their influence territories and medium territories. The Gezi Movement and the Green Movement took place inside the empire states. The Syrian uprisings and Bahrain Human Rights Movement broke out inside influence territories, whereas the Egyptian, Tunisian and Libyan revolutions erupted outside the empire states of the region, their territories and medium territories. Although all of these movements took place within the states of emergency and because of that the majority of them have failed to replace that state and structure with a new one, they also seem different, among other things, in terms of violence, goal, extent and level of success. Such categorisation helps us understand the reason why some of them became revolutionary whereas other remained reformist; why some of them are brutally suppressed, while others have succeeded to initially reach their goals; why some of them have been deformed, burst into violence and fragmentation and factionalism, while others became silent.

The Iranian Green Movement of 2009 erupted against the fraudulent elections, in which Mahmoud Ahmadinejad was claimed to be the president elect. Nevertheless, these protests did not challenge the elections only. They initially targeted the structural developments started since the conservatives first took over in 2005.[18] The 2009 uprisings took place in the midst of the solidification and accumulation process. Therefore, the government was determined to prevent the reformists from taking over, since this could disrupt the continuity of the process. A few days before the uprisings, key reformist figures along with several journalists and civil and political activists have been arrested, election headquarters were attacked by the police and plain clothes, and numerous websites, newspapers, journals and party headquarters were shut down. With the escalation of the uprisings, people not only chanted against Ahmadinejad, the IRGC and the Supreme Leader, but also Iran's involvement in Lebanon and Palestine.

Similar trends are visible in Turkey's Gezi Movement of 2013. The Gezi Movement erupted against crony capitalism of the regime and confiscation of the public space by private capital in order to construct a shopping mall.[19] The protests not only contested the urban development plan of Istanbul, but also the authoritarianism of Erdoğan's government and his regime's involvement in Syria. Similar to Iran, over-accumulation of Turkey seemed to have played a significant role in solidification of the regime and its political involvement in the region. The Gezi movement not only challenged the state's endeavours to change urban life according to neoliberal policies of the AK party, but also the regime's engagement in Syria.

On the other hand, the Syrian uprisings and the Bahrain's Human Rights Movement erupted within the influence territories of Iran and Saudi Arabia as two competing empire states of the region, particularly after the miraculous over-accumulation of the recent years. These two movements are different when their goals and forms of collective actions are concerned. Whereas the anti-Assad oppositions became increasingly violent, Bahrain's Human Rights Movement remained mostly non-violent. And unlike the Syrian opposition movement, Bahrain's Human Rights Movement did not practically pursue regime change. However, both of them have been brutally suppressed by the government with the help of outside support. The Syrian uprisings have not only threatened the state of emergency of the Assad Regime, but also the territorial interests of Iran and Russia, of which Syria is a close ally. Parallel events took place in Bahrain as a close ally of Saudi Arabia and a member of the Arab League and the GCC. When uprisings erupted in Bahrain, they were attributed to Iran's intervention, which was a good excuse to suppress non-violent demands.

This framework seems also useful to understand other political protest movements such as the Palestinian Intifada and the Ukraine's Maydan. Whereas the Intifada has been suppressed by the Israeli government supported by western powers, Ukraine's movement ended up with sectarian clashes of the rival groups in the middle of competition of the two major empires, the Russian Federation and the European Union.

The final category of the movements includes North African protest movements particularly those of Egypt and Tunisia. In both cases, the revolutionary protests have initially succeeded in overthrowing the regime, partially thanks to the support of western powers, although the consequences are very challenging, particularly concerning Egypt. The initial triumph of these revolutions was, among other things, rooted in their position being relatively outside the territory of the three mentioned competing empire states.

Protest Movements in the State of Emergency

Although recent protest movements challenged the state of emergency in one way or another, they also seem to suffer from some of the characteristics of the emergency state. As soon as they were framed they became fragmented, and while being temporary, emergent and extraordinary, they were exclusivist tending to escape leadership and organisational mobilisation, and became fuzzy in tactics and aims. More important, whereas they were initially very political, at the end of the day they became de-politicised, if not anti-political. For instance, compared to the Iranian reform movement of the 1990s, the Green Movement was more challenging for the regime, more unthinkable and more extraordinary. It benefited from Internet technologies and new means of communication. It was also privileged by being much more documented, recorded and narrated compared to the previous movements. Nonetheless, contrary to the reform movement, the participants were ambiguous about plans and purposes. Therefore, they soon became fragmented around issues such as leadership, plan and organisation. The Green Movement was initially more political than the reform movement, but it ended up with being almost de-politicised. Consequently, at the end, many participants found themselves much more individuated, atomised, hopeless and disappointed than before.

Framing protest movements had become more challenging than before considering the deterioration of life conditions as a result of neoliberal and imperialist policies of the regimes, escalation of state's surveillance and finally regrouping of the conservative forces in various countries. This is despite democratisation of the Middle Eastern societies becoming much urgent than before. Yet, one cannot avoid asking whether protest movements will emerge in the future, whether they are doomed to failure, or whether they will be able to replace the state of emergency and its neoliberal expansionist and authoritarian policies with new kind of think and action.

A main challenge vis-à-vis protest movements of the Middle East is how to create inclusive solidarities beyond identity divisions and local communities that are able to challenge the hegemony of the state of emergency and its neoliberal imperialist expansion. Such framing requires specific plans for action and certain goals such as re-nationalisation. However, this seems to be impossible without building up solidarities beyond national borders. The state of emergency is not after all legitimised by itself and is not restricted to a given society. As manifested earlier, it is rather invigorated by global hegemonic trends, although it might take a specific shape in a given society. This situation is not restricted to a few societies of the region; it tends to expand in time and space and infiltrate into different territories. The more this situation expands, the more it becomes hegemonic. Therefore, unless there are cross-border solidarities beyond local, national and regional identities the hegemony of the state of emergency cannot be interrupted effectively.

Notes

1. Andrej Zwitter, "Arab Spring, State of Emergency, and Constitutional Reform," in *Air and Space Power Journal (ASPJ)*, vol. 5, issue 2, (2013), p. 48. For the state of emergency in Tunisia and Libya, see also Andrej Zwitter, "Egypt's State of Emergency Revisited," at http://constitutional-change.com/egypts-state-of-emergency-revisited/
2. Andrej Zwitter, "Arab Spring, ..."; Andreij Zwitter, "Egypt's State of Emergency Revisited," at http://constitutional-change.com/egypts-state-of-emergency-revisited/
3. Hesham Salam, "Letting Go of Revolutionary Purity," at http://www.jadaliyya.com/pages/index/16167/letting-go-of-revolutionary-purity
4. Anna Borshchevskaya, "Sponsored Corruption and Neglected Reform in Syria," in *Middle East Quarterly*, vol. 17, no. 3, 2010, pp. 42, 45.
5. Transparency International 2008; Borshchevskaya, ibid., p. 41.
6. Felix Imonti, "Egypt: As Military owns 92 Percent, Land Reform is Key," at http://oilprice.com/Geopolitics/Africa/Egypt-for-Sale.htmlImonti, 2013
7. Asef Bayat, *Life as Politics: How Ordinary People Change the Middle East* (Amsterdam University Press: 2010), chapter 9.
8. Imonti, ibid.
9. Theorists of imperialism associate it with expansion, although they define expansion differently and from various perspectives. Lenin viewed Imperialism as the highest form of capitalism and capitalist accumulation. However, Edward Said viewed it more as a cultural territorial expansion. Hanah Arendt, on the other hand, defines imperialism as expansion for expansion's sake, whereas David Harvey associates Imperialism not only with territorial, but also over-accumulation and expansion in time and space. Expansion is not restricted only to empire states. Friedrich Ratzel, the classic geopolitician, associated expansion with the state as well. He suggested that even a state had to grow, to expand, and to establish living frontiers or borders that were dynamic and subject to change. Borders become insignificant in that a developing state or one that is advancing is likely to require annexation of territories that are controlled by other less powerful states. See Lenin, *Imperialism: The Highest Stage of Capitalism*; Edward Said, *Culture and Imperialism* (New York: Vintage Books, 1993); Hanah Arendt, *Imperialism* (Houghton

Mifflin Harcourt, 1968); David Harvey, *The New Imperialism* (Oxford University Press, 2003).

10. Harvey, ibid., pp. 102-3.
11. Mohammad Maljoo, "Political Consequence of Privatisation," at http://pecritique.com/2013/11/05 /پیامد- سیاسی- خصوصی-سازی- محمد-مالجو/
12. *Time,* November 14, 2014, at http://time.com/3584585/saudi-arabia-bulldozes-over-its-heritage/
13. *Independent*, March 15, 2013, at http://www.independent.co.uk/news/world/middle-east/the-photos-saudi-arabia-doesnt-want-seen--and-proof-islams-most-holy-relics-are-being-demolished-in-mecca-8536968.html
14. http://english.alarabiya.net/en/News/middle-east/2014/10/13/126-mosques-to-be-razed-in-Saudi-Arabia-for-Madinah-mosque-expansion.html
15. *The Guardian*, March 9, 2015, at http://www.theguardian.com/world/2015/mar/09/saudi-arabia-becomes-worlds-biggest-arms-importer
16. See also Ziauddin Sardar, *Mecca: The Sacred City* (Bloomsbury: 2014), particularly chapter 10.
17. Murat Cem Mengüç, "Istanbul, Its People, and Their Limits," at http://www.jadaliyya.com/pages/index/13841/istanbul-its-people-and-their-limits;
    Elvan Erik, Bio-Istanbul: A Speculative, segregationist, and Sustainable Urbanism," at http://www.jadaliyya.com/pages/index/20861/bio-istanbul_a-speculative-segregationist-and-sust
18. Fatemeh Sadeghi, "A Struggle Against Islamist Patriarchy? Women and the Green Movement," in Negin Nabavi (ed.), *From Theocracy to the Green Movement* (Palgrave Macmillan: 2012), pp. 123-36.
19. Nilüfer Göle, "Anatomy of a Public Square Movement," in *Insight Turkey*, vol. 15, 2013, pp. 7-14.

9. Ruminations on the Characteristics and Consequences of Political Protests in the Arab World

Ranjit Gupta

Distinctive Characteristics of the Arab World

Historical Background

The contemporary Arab world embraces 22 countries extending from Mauritania on the Atlantic coast to Iraq, along the Persian Gulf, bordering Iran; and, dipping into Africa proper to include Sudan, Eritrea and Djibouti. An interesting point to note is that the contemporary, conventionally understood "Arab world" has a long lineage, most of it already having come into existence way back in the first half of the seventh century AD after the advent of Islam when Arab culture, language, people and religion spread outwards from the central Arabian Peninsula through conquest and trade.

The year AD 622 marks the birth of Islam when the Prophet migrated from Mecca with his followers to Medina where he was very enthusiastically received. After his death, during the period of the first four Caliphs, known as the Rashidun or the Righteous Ones, Islam spread with extraordinary speed and spectacular success. In less than 30 years most of the territory of the Persian Empire, the modern Levant and coastal North Africa up to present-day Fez in Morocco on the Atlantic coast, including Egypt and all the territory in-between, became a part of Arab domains. The map below shows the extent of the Rashidun Empire at its peak. A point to note is that Islam thus expanded mainly through the sword in what emerged as the "Arab world" and later also into different parts of Eurasia contiguous to and with West Asia.

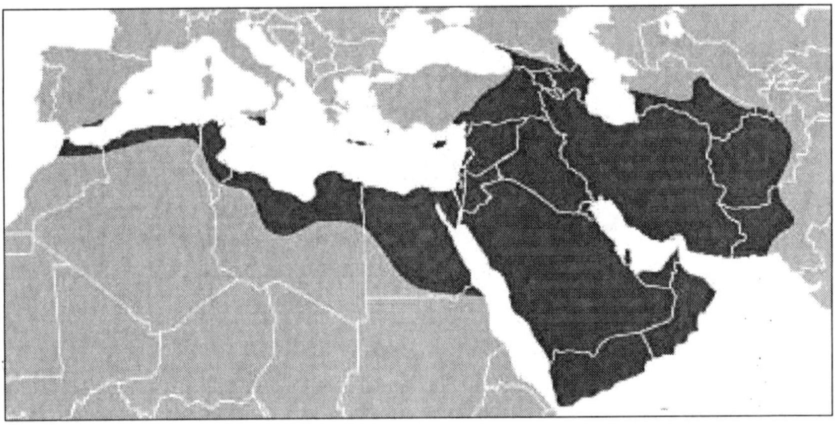

This was soon followed by the Arab (Moorish) conquest of Spain. The enlightened rule of the Abbasid dynasty marked the Arab Golden Age. Historians usually date this period from about AD 750 to 1250. The Arab world thus has had a glorious and rich past.

Anger amongst Christians was building up due to the growing challenge of Arab Muslims to Christendom and to the Constantinople-based Byzantine Christian Empire. It was greatly heightened by the destruction of Christendom's holiest site, the Church of the Holy Sepulchre, under orders of Fatimid Caliph Al-Hakim bin-Amr Allah on October 18, 1009, which Caliph Omar and early Muslim rulers had protected. The increasing anger finally resulted in the Crusades triggered in particular by the capture of Jerusalem in 1076. Though ultimately defeated, the Crusades initiated the processes of the decline of the Arab world. They were followed by the Mongol invasion. On February 13, 1258 Baghdad—the then greatest city in the Middle East—fell and its treasure was looted, magnificent mosques were destroyed, and the population massacred.

Thereafter the Arabs came under the Ottoman Empire. With its defeat in World War I, the British and the French carved its Arab domains into countries with arbitrary borders and apportioned them amongst themselves—the Sykes Picot project—to serve their imperial interests, abandoning the promises of independence that had been held out. It is significant that no Arab country was amongst original members of the League of Nations. The Arab world was thus dealt another blow.

Their situation worsened even further after World War II. The West's creation of Israel in the Arab heartland and Israel's inexorable territorial expansion thereafter inflicting a string of military defeats on the Arabs, has left the Arab psyche particularly deeply scarred with a debilitating sense of victimhood.

Contemporary Socio-Political Realities

Given this historical background and having rulers, many of them perceived to be lackeys of the West, has been fuelling growing feelings of anger, rage, revenge and vengeance amongst Arab peoples. This sentiment is compounded further by the fact that Arab countries have never known anything other than autocratic regimes and abysmally poor governance.

The Arab world is overwhelmingly Muslim—except for Egypt with 89% Muslims and Lebanon with only 54% Muslims, all other Arab countries have a Muslim population of over 96%. They constitute an "Ummah," a community which, in theory, is supposed to transcend national loyalties and national borders. Given their common language and religion and shared ethno-historical legacy, all this results in happenings in one Arab country tending to evoke huge popular resonance in other Arab countries.

A unique characteristic of Arab culture and social organisation is the immensely large role that religion plays in almost every aspect of daily life of all strata of people in the Arab world. Islam also puts serious restrictions on the things that people can or cannot do and breach thereof could evoke strong punitive reactions. Praying is a communal exercise.

An emphasis on religious values and a return to traditionalism are increasingly evident in public discourse, appearance and behaviour. Involvement of large numbers of people in favour of or against particular activities or entities is much easier to organise if such activity is seen to have or can be accorded religious connotations since the overwhelming majority of Arab people are conservative and deeply religious. All these factors cumulatively provide Islamist groupings a natural anchor and reservoir of popular resonance, support and sympathy.

The Ikhwan al-Muslimeen or Muslim Brotherhood was founded in Egypt in 1928. Branches were established in all Arab countries and indeed in most Muslim countries. This organisation became the foundational cornerstone and initial inspiration for most of the subsequent Islamist movements. The founder, Hassan al-Banna (1906-49), rejected Western notions of secular governance and rule, postulating that without religious governance the Muslim world would be "a society of cultural mongrels and spiritual half-castes ... Politics is part of religion," he wrote. "Caesar and what belongs to Caesar is for God Almighty alone; Islam commanded a unity of life; to impose upon Islam the Christian separation of loyalties [into church and state] is to deny it its essential meaning and very existence." This interpretation is acquiring increasing public support by the day across the Arab world.

Wahhabism, which predates the Muslim Brotherhood, has been sedulously promoted by Saudi Arabia in particular for decades throughout the Islamic world in general and in the Arab world in particular. Operating in an increasingly more fertile environment, this doctrine provided the basic ideological foundations for the birth, growth and spread of nostalgic harking back to the pristine Islam of the Prophet and his companions, which is the essence of Salafism. In the hands of extremists all this has resulted in increasing radicalism and violent militancy.

In democratic countries strong civil society institutions try to ensure that governments cannot violate public trust without political costs. However, truly meaningful civil society institutions are virtually non-existent in most Arab countries. In the oil-rich GCC countries the state provides generous welfare in exchange for unquestioning public obedience, buying peace and stability through this via media. How long this lasts remains to be seen. In the less well-off Arab countries, which constitute the majority of Arab countries, authoritarian, secular regimes ensured obedience through straightforward authoritarian methods. The delivery of public services and welfare was mired in corruption and particularly ineffective in the rural areas and the poorer sections of urban agglomerations where the overwhelming majority of people live. Religion oriented entities such as the Muslim Brotherhood filled this void by becoming a far more effective agency to provide such services to the people at large thus garnering enduring and widespread grass-roots public support for themselves. In this changing milieu, the failure of the authoritarian secular model produced convulsions that almost naturally catapulted Islamists to the fore.

These overarching factors distinguish the Arab world from all other regional groupings and have contributed to the emergence of a new political actor, multinational activist Islamist groups, many of them increasingly militant and armed. In this essay the phrase "Islamist groups" is used to mean all groups and entities whose engagement in political activities, violent or non-violent, is articulated through Islam-based or related actions and discourse. These Islamic militants seem to be able to travel between Arab countries quite easily and, though non-Arab but a Muslim country, Turkey—in the past 3 years the pre-eminent patron of fundamentalist Islam together with Qatar—has been the most prominent gateway for militant Islamists' ingress into West Asia, in particular Syria. This religion infused easy multinational cross-border movement and togetherness in activity has become a natural, unhindered process within the Arab world. A physical "Ummah" seems to be in the making adding strength to this heretofore rather metaphorical concept.

Broad-Brush Consideration of the Nature of Political Protest in the Arab World

Political protest can broadly be defined as the articulation or manifestation of dissent, objection, opposition and resistance to the actions and policies of incumbent governments. In democratic countries Parliament, free media, activities of political parties, an independent judiciary and appeals to courts, NGOs and civil society institutions, demonstrations, trade unions, strikes, sit-ins, etc., are amongst instrumentalities through which protests are articulated or manifested.

Political protest can also be motivated by dissatisfaction with and consequent desire to change existing political and governance structures and mechanisms; this can be brought about through prescribed constitutional means such as referenda, no-confidence motions, constitutional amendments, etc.

Furthermore, Governments derive their legitimacy through the electoral process which is a regular periodic exercise. Public unhappiness with the actions and policies of incumbent governments can be expressed by electorally defeating the political party which had constituted a particular government thus bringing about a change of government. All these constitute traditional constitutional approaches.

However, these modalities of political protest can operate, primarily, if not only, in respect of countries which are functioning democracies in which the norms, processes and architecture of governance are in accordance with a voluntarily accepted Constitution. The Arab world constitutes a distinct socio-political grouping with the greatest democracy deficit; functionally, it is an island of autocracies though most have Constitutions, so-called elections and parliaments, shuras, etc., which are really window dressing.

In the Arab world the monarch or dictator or effective leader or ruler, by whatever name he may be called, and his handpicked coterie decide all government policies for all practical purposes and it is in the ruler's power and discretion to determine or manipulate how the people can interact with the government, if at all; the people have no intrinsic or effective institutional voice in influencing, changing or challenging such top-down governance and enactments.

Normatively, authoritarianism implicitly but inevitably encourages violent resistance because the more normal forms of peaceful dissent, protest and resistance are either institutionally impaired or substantively unavailable and/or are perceived to be ineffective in obtaining redress and desired results. Therefore, ultimately, protest inevitably takes the form of violent insurrection to overthrow or at least subvert the regime. The State reacts with violence of its own and this process locks both the protesters and the State in a vicious cycle of escalating violence on both sides. This leads to another characteristic of protests in the Arab world, particularly in the post 9/11 scenario, in that this violence, sooner or later, but inevitably, gets deeply intertwined with religion and matters of faith; much of all such violence is increasingly very clearly being given a religion related justification. In the Arab world due to the long-standing schism between Shia and Sunni such violence, both by the protesters and by the State, is also often directed against specific sections of the population, or even randomly and indiscriminately against the civilian population at large. The religion factor also makes suppression of such protests relatively riskier and dangerous as this further polarises populations between different sects on the one hand, and contributes to further strengthening support for militant religious groups, which have sprouted in large numbers in the past 15 years, on the other.

All this has contributed to the emergence of a new, frightening, political phenomenon—multinational militant Islam operating transnationally to fight forces perceived to be intrinsically anti-Islam and targeting regimes of more than one state simultaneously; it is creating havoc in the Arab world.

In an increasingly globalised and interconnected world, alarmed by these developments and socio-political trends, foreign countries, including Arab countries, have been intervening both militarily and through the exercise of all other available economic, ideological and political leverages in the internal affairs of selected Arab countries. Such foreign intervention has further accentuated sentiments of aggravation and has made Islamic militants all the more determined to impose their vision of appropriate governance in Arab countries in particular, and Islamic countries in general. They increasingly believe that this can only be achieved by completely dismantling the existing political architecture and creating absolutely new and different political ground realities throughout the Arab world, thus imparting "political protest" an altogether new dimension and taking it to an unprecedentedly different higher level.

The "Arab Spring"—A False Dawn

Arab countries have never known anything other than autocratic regimes. For generations Arabs have lived with them without the means or possibilities of any fundamental political change. Protests in the past were relatively easily suppressed. In the winter of 2010/spring of 2011 people rose up spontaneously and absolutely unprecedentedly in the hundreds of thousands day after day in Tunisia and Egypt demanding not merely reform but regime change. In the Arab context this was REVOLUTION in capital letters. This was a larger than anything that had happened in Arab history. There has been no rational explanation why this eruption took place at the time it did and for the sudden realisation by the common people that their destiny is in their own hands and will no longer be permitted to be determined by their dictatorial rulers or by foreigners since the ostensible triggers, in particular the economic ones, have existed for decades. Before regimes can be overthrown or dislodged, people must overcome fear of regimes, even of the most autocratic ones and must even be ready to die. Astonishingly, this happened! Once again, there is no rational explanation of why and how at that particular time.

There were several other unique features of this popular upsurge of iconic protest—it started without known or easily identifiable leaders, without the banner of any specific ideology or organisation, without instigation and incitement from abroad. It was pre-eminently a movement spearheaded by the younger generation and was consciously inclusive of all the diverse elements that constitute a national society. Unprecedentedly extensive use of new social media—Facebook, Twitter, YouTube, Internet generally, etc.—sending messages motivating and galvanising protesters in the instantaneous mobilisation of hundreds of thousands of protesters at predetermined locations rapidly on the one hand, and greatly complicating regime responses on the other.

The unrest initially began everywhere as a peaceful, non-violent protest against autocratic, corrupt and brazenly repressive rule and the lack of economic development and opportunity for the people at large while the ruling elite lived in luxury. The focus of the protests was almost completely domestic—a demand for democracy, for fundamental political, economic and social reform, for basic human dignity and freedoms and had little or nothing to do with external relations. Despite their ubiquitous and effective intelligence services, the governments of Egypt and Tunisia were taken completely by surprise; indeed, governments across the Arab world also. In the rest of the world also no government, no intelligence agency, no expert on the Arab world had anticipated even the remote possibility of anything like this happening.

Most of the leaders and a high proportion of the fighters of Al Qaeda were Arabs but very significantly, there was no Islamist fervour or flavour to these protests, which clearly represented a more than tacit rejection of what Al Qaeda has stood for. Despite its popularity in the Arab street and its immediate support of the revolts in Tunisia, Egypt and Libya, Iran was not heralded as a beacon. In fact, foreign policy issues had not been a factor at all in initiating, propelling or sustaining the protests; there was a conspicuous absence of anti-Americanism and anti-Israeli sentiment.

Though this uplifting spirit of revolt against autocratic authority provided a common thread that underlay the unrest which spread across the Arab world like wildfire, very distinct variations in the subsequent evolution of events in each country emerged including in regard to the approach adopted by the people, reactions by ruling regimes and policies of outside powers.

Without taking anything away from the courageous protests of hundreds of thousands of common people, the unvarnished reality is that the regimes in Egypt and Tunisia fell because the armed forces chose not to violently confront their own people and thus effectively deprived the two regimes of the only major potential instrument of overcoming the revolts; the dictators, being utterly unpopular and deeply despised, had no legs to stand on to survive. Protests also broke out in Bahrain, Libya, Oman, Syria and Yemen. A truly miraculous "Arab Spring" had seemingly dawned.

However, rulers in other Arab countries carefully observed evolving events and drew lessons from the outcomes in Egypt and Tunisia where strongly entrenched dictators in power for decades fell within just weeks. Regime preservation became the major obsession and pre-eminent priority of the ruling classes, immaterial of the costs in blood, treasure and innocent lives that would inevitably be lost in the process. In many countries, the ruler's family members and close tribal kin commanded and controlled the intelligence services, the internal security apparatus and the military which made quashing the protests much easier. In just a few months the soaring hopes of a jasmine scented spring gave way to a summer of growing discontent and frustration amidst harsh and bloody repression of popular uprisings as the regimes struck back with brutal force leading to still continuing civil wars in Libya, Syria and Yemen, including regime change in Libya and Yemen. The protests were squashed in Bahrain by a show of overwhelming force but tensions persist strongly under the surface. Protest in Oman was not directed against the popular and respected Sultan but more against governmental corruption and economic distress. The Sultan dismissed most of his long-serving and senior Ministers, and helped by a generous grant by Saudi Arabia announced economic sops.

Foreign intervention including by Arab countries became an integral part of unfolding events. Thousands of armed Islamic militants poured in from foreign countries, particularly into Syria, to make a messy situation significantly worse. Western countries conned the Security Council to approve R2P intervention in Libya which turned out to be a fig leaf for regime change. The situation for the Libyan people is infinitely worse than it had been under Gaddafi and the country is now a conglomeration of 21 different emirates controlled by different warring Islamic militant groups and tribal warlords with two weak, ineffectual contending ostensible central governments and parliaments. It will take decades for stability to return; peace talks between the rival "governments" and contending militant groups under UN auspices rhetorically welcomed by all countries have little chance of success unless the foreign patrons of different groups get involved.

Syria has been completely ravaged by a devastating and destructive civil war in which several dozens of armed militant Islamic groups are fighting against each other and against the Assad regime which has been reacting brutally carrying out indiscriminate attacks against perceived opposition strongholds; a supposedly secular largely ineffective Syrian National Army is also a part of the mix of rebel groups. Over 220,000 have died and almost half the population of the country has been displaced from their homes, villages and cities. The Syrian conflict has reached these horrendous proportions to a very great extent due to overt Qatari, Saudi and Turkish intervention and Western support, with the conflict deliberately being imparted a sectarian character; later Assad contributed his bit too. Peace talks under Russian and UN auspices between the government and myriad opposition groups rhetorically welcomed by all countries are unlikely to succeed unless the foreign patrons of contending parties are involved.

In Egypt, even though the people had achieved their aim of the hated dictator Mubarak being overthrown, it was the military that grabbed power and ruled for the next one year. Having tasted success, the people forced the new Supreme Council of the Armed Forces regime to hold elections which unsurprisingly resulted in a Muslim Brotherhood government; having struggled and failed for 8 decades in achieving power through both constitutional and violent means, when power finally came unexpectedly, the Brotherhood foolishly launched immediately upon the implementation of its Islamist agenda; in an irony of ironies, the Army prodded by enthusiastic public approval—the demonstrators even outnumbered those that had protested against Mubarak—overthrew President Morsi and elected the Army chief as the new president by an overwhelming majority. His government is even more autocratic than the Mubarak dictatorship had been. Muslim Brotherhood leaders, members and supporters are being hunted and hounded with unprecedented harshness; the judiciary is hand in glove with the government and has been handing out death sentences to hundreds of Brotherhood members. The entity has been declared a terrorist organisation and banned while Mubarak, his cronies and his sons have been exonerated of all charges. The prominent figures steering the Arab Spring protests in 2011 are either in prison, exile or have renounced political activity in sheer disgust. The past two years have witnessed an enormous increase in terrorist attacks within Egypt by Islamist elements, most of them ascribed as belonging to the Muslim Brotherhood. In the Sinai Peninsula there is an Al Qaeda linked group—"Ansar Bayt(Bait) al-Maqdis," which is responsible for a continuing spate of terrorist attacks particularly on security forces inflicting fairly heavy casualties; it has recently pledged allegiance to the Islamic State.

The situations in Libya, Syria and Yemen have gone far beyond protest and have become full-fledged civil wars. I do not see an early end to the conflicts in Libya, Syria or Yemen; meaningful stability is a long way off in all three countries. Yemen is also facing the spectre of secession of the South because the central government is so weak. The situation in Egypt is in some ways even worse than what it was before the advent of the so-called Arab Spring and it remains to be seen whether democracy will come to Egypt anytime soon.

After Ben Ali's overthrow, Al-Nahda leaders returned to Tunisia from exile in Europe and quickly took top spot in the emerging political firmament. Impressively, a new Constitution was adopted while Al-Nahda was sharing power; it is the only Constitution in the Arab world which does not mention Sharia as the source of law and legislation, with this decision being a conscious and deliberate choice. In spite of being the overwhelmingly largest party in Parliament, Al-Nahda voluntarily stepped down in favour of a government of technocrats in January 2014 in response to public and civil society demands. In the subsequent second elections a secular party has won beating Al-Nahda into second place and Al-Nahda has gracefully accepted defeat but suggested formation of a national unity government in the overall interests of the country. Tunisia has been the sole success story of the hope that had dawned in the winter of 2010-2011 perhaps because it has the highest human development indicators and the most emancipated societal fabric in the Arab world. It is the only exception to the chaos that has been spreading elsewhere and exhibits that an alternative to authoritarianism and militancy is quite possible even in today's Arab world. This achievement is all the more impressive because Islamic militants have been quite active in Tunisia too and there are large numbers of Tunisian jihadis fighting in Syria.

Even though they were neither in the vanguard nor even active participants, the single most significant long-term fallout of the so-called "Arab Spring" has been the emergence of armed militant Islamist groups as the main defining political actor in the Arab world. Except in Tunisia, political Islam has received a serious setback. However, fear of regimes has begun to be exorcised from the Arab psyche and this is a permanent gain and authoritarian regimes must bear this in mind.

Emergence and Rise of Militant Islamist Movements

West Asia has been a particularly volatile region since World War II witnessing numerous wars and much conflict, both within countries and between countries. The first 15 years of this millennium have been the worst from this perspective. Contentious discourse and armed conflict within and between states, extremism, foreign interventions, sectarianism, terrorist attacks and violence of the most brutal kind seem to have now become the new normal for the region, typified particularly by the emergence, beliefs and practices of the Islamic State. The depredations of contemporary armed militant Islamist entities are the embodiment of a unique and hugely destructive form of "political protest" which has become endemic in the Arab world. There are now literally hundreds of extremist groups big and small, but the two major ones are briefly discussed below.

Al Qaeda

The main architects of the military response to the Soviet invasion and occupation of Afghanistan were the United States, Saudi Arabia and Pakistan and their chosen tool was the creation of a multinational army of mujahideen—jihadi warriors—fired up by Islamic fervour to combat the atheist communists in what has been dubbed the "modern jihad." They succeeded spectacularly resulting in Soviet withdrawal from Afghanistan, which started on May 15, 1988 and also precipitated internal processes in the USSR that contributed to the disintegration of the Soviet Union itself. Emboldened by victory over a superpower and considering it a victory of Islam—a rare event after a very long period of repeated military setbacks by Arab and Muslim countries and peoples—jihad became both a major inspiration and tool for emerging hardline Islamist elements in the Arab world in particular. A new entity Al Qaeda was formed at a meeting on August 11, 1988 convened by Osama bin Laden, a Saudi, and Ayman Zawahiri and Dr. Fadl, both Egyptians, in Peshawar, Pakistan.

The Iraqi invasion and occupation of Kuwait in 1990 had led to a Saudi invitation to the Americans to end the Iraqi aggression and defend the Kingdom against a possible Iraqi attack. The process involved a peak presence of 550,000 US troops on Saudi soil. These developments caused the emergence of a radical Islamist movement in Saudi Arabia in particular and in the Arab world as a whole. Osama bin Laden, who had just returned to the Kingdom from Afghanistan, left Saudi Arabia for Sudan in mid-1991 when the Saudi royal family denied him permission to conduct a jihad against the Iraqis occupying Kuwait. He mobilised jihadi veterans there which led to the cancelling of his Saudi citizenship in March 1994. Thereafter bin Laden issued several communiqués denouncing Saudi Arabian policies. On August 23, 1996 Osama published his "Declaration of Jihad against the

Americans who are occupying the Land of the Two Holy Places" calling for a "Global Jihad" against the US, the West and their puppet regimes in the Arab world. In 1996, the Pakistani intelligence agency, ISI, introduced Osama bin Laden to Mullah Omar, thus setting the stage for a symbiotic relationship developing with the Taliban—it provided bin Laden with security and protection, while the latter reinforced the Taliban forces with a few thousand Al Qaeda fighters.

Since 1992 terrorist attacks against American targets in particular and in several Arab countries have been taking place with increasing frequency with large-scale civilian casualties also; the high point of Al Qaeda's jihad on the West was the spectacular destruction of the World Trade Centre in New York on September 11, 2001. All this constituted militant Islamists' protests against the West and their lackeys in the Arab world, in the only way they could retaliate against the armed might of the West and the authoritarianism of Arab rulers and dictators, exhibiting a new and still continuing response to decades of humiliation of the Arabs.

Branches of Al Qaeda have emerged in several countries, the most prominent being Al Qaeda in the Arabian Peninsula (AQAP), created in Saudi Arabia but later moving to Yemen where it is particularly active; Al Qaeda in the Arab Maghreb headquartered in Algeria with branches active in Libya and also stretching into Africa particularly Mali; Al Shabaab in Somalia; and the Jabhat Al-Nusra in Syria. Hundreds of other myriad Islamist militant groups have sprouted particularly in the Arab world but also in countries like Afghanistan and Pakistan, even Bangladesh, and are beginning to emerge in India and South-east Asian countries also.

The Islamic State

The Islamic State represents the most extreme manifestation of protest in the Arab world; if it succeeds that would spell the end of the state system in West Asia with potentially disastrous implications for the world at large.

An account of how and why it emerged would be in order. America's unilateral, unprovoked and completely unjustified invasion of Iraq in 2003 and its subsequent military occupation of Iraq provided a further and enormous push to the rise of militant Islam.

The historical reality that Iraq has always been ruled by Sunnis was dramatically upended by US Governor of Iraq Paul Bremmer's first two decrees which ordered the wholesale dismantling both of the Baathist Party, which was virtually synonymous with the State, and of the Iraqi Army. Demobilised and suddenly and sullenly unemployed thousands of Iraqi army personnel, including skilled Saddam-era officers, joined insurgent militias, greatly strengthening newly sprouting anti-government forces, while simultaneously the new government was stripped of its administrative and military capabilities. The Sunnis were deeply angry. Saddam's unnecessary humiliation compounded the anger. Since 2006 Iraq has been ruled by a Shia government under US installed and supported Nuri al Maliki that has been particularly brazen in implementing an enlarging sectarian agenda, contributing to the total alienation of the Sunni population of the country. The Shia-Sunni divide has never been as poisonous as it has become in the last few years. A Sunni backlash was inevitable.

This inevitably led to the outbreak of Sunni insurgencies spearheaded by the newly formed Al Qaeda in Iraq (AQI) established by the Jordanian radical Abu Musab al-Zarqawi, leading to the overwhelmingly Sunni inhabited Anbar province and parts of Baghdad descending into anarchy between 2005 and 2008. At its peak level of influence in 2006-7 the AQI had taken over significant chunks of Sunni Iraq and even set up a quasi-government along harsh Islamic lines in some of the areas it controlled. This finally led to the Sunni population at large revolting out of anger with AQI's brutal rule. This revolt, dubbed the Anbar Awakening, named after the province in which it began, resulted in former Sunni insurgents and the general Sunni populace implausibly partnering even with the hated Americans and the equally hated new Shia dominated Iraqi military to uproot the AQI. The fall of AQI illustrated clearly that extremism will fail if it does not have the support of common Sunni Iraqis. The Iraqi government failed to grasp the self-evident and clear implications of this simple, common-sense message that was sent out. Had the Maliki government not gratuitously alienated the Sahwa, as the Sunni or Anbar Awakening Movement was called locally, almost 100,000 strong, Iraq may have remained relatively peaceful.

Meanwhile, defeated then, the AQI retreated to and regrouped in Syria and mutated into the Islamic State of Iraq and Syria (ISIS) and returned to Iraq in early 2014 with devastating success rapidly overrunning northern Iraq and capturing towns at will including Mosul, Iraq's second largest city, on June 10.

On June 30 the ISIS announced the establishment of an Islamic Caliphate to be ruled strictly in accordance with the Sharia, and its leader Abu Bakr al-Baghdadi was declared the new Caliph Ibrahim, the leader of Muslims everywhere. He was a detainee of the US at Camp Bucca, the thousands of detainees there were to form the core of the ISIS—"If there was no American prison in Iraq, there would be no IS now. Bucca was a factory. It made us all. It built our ideology. … We had so much time to sit and plan," he continued. "It was the perfect environment. We all agreed to get together when we got out. The way to reconnect was easy." Initially, Al Qaeda in Iraq and the Ba'athists had been fierce ideological enemies, but the rising power of the Shias—and their backers in Iran—brought them together ("ISIS: The Inside Story," Martin Chulov, quoting former senior ISIS commander Abu Ahmed in the *Manchester Guardian*, December 11, 2014).

Baghdadi was released in December 2004 and was thereafter a part of the Al Qaeda hierarchy until expelled by Zawahiri. The ISIS has been renamed as the "Islamic State"—this name now stands both for the organisation and the territory that it controls, which comprises two-fifths of the total territory of Syria and two-fifths of the total territory of Iraq, erasing the boundary between these two countries, and stretching from near Aleppo along Syria's boundaries with Turkey into Iraq, incorporating its Sunni populated regions to the outskirts of Baghdad and along the boundaries with Jordan and northern Saudi Arabia. It holds assets of several billion—cash taken from all the banks and government treasuries of the towns it has taken over in Syria and Iraq; ransom money from those kidnapped including almost $135 million reportedly paid by European governments or companies to secure the release of their kidnapped nationals; from sale of ancient antiquities; revenues of $ 3 million per day from sale of oil and oil products from the 11 oilfields in Syria and Iraq and two refineries that it controls; from fees and taxes; from funding from entities and individuals in Gulf countries; looting from businessmen and common citizens in territories that it controls, etc. It is virtually self-sufficient economically and financially. It is very well-equipped militarily having captured huge amounts of sophisticated weaponry abandoned by the Iraqi army; and in Syria captured from the rebels which was supplied by the West and GCC countries. It is running a full-fledged administration. In recent months thousands of supporters have joined the Islamic State forces taking numbers of fighters way beyond the earlier estimates of a hard core of about 10-12,000 fighters in Iraq, mostly Iraqi, and perhaps thrice as many in Syria, majority Syrian, but with at least one-third being foreigners, including many from Western countries. A major reason for success has been the support of local Sunni populations. US Secretary of Defence Chuck Hagel said on August 22, "this is beyond anything that we've seen." It is more powerful than Al Qaeda, which never explicitly ruled territory, and even the Taliban, which was essentially a creation of and dependent on Pakistan, and far more brutal than either.

The Islamic State has declared war against the US in particular and the West in general; it has also declared war against pro-West Arab regimes particularly Saudi Arabia, the bastion of Sunni conservatism. Interestingly, it has in addition declared war against all other Islamist militant groups including, in particular, Al Qaeda. Its ideology demands the extermination of the heretic Shias and other "minorities." Despite all this it has been showing continuing resilience, but for how long?

The Way Ahead

The world has no option but to defeat the Islamic State; otherwise not only West Asia but its neighbours and even further afield, for example, Europe from where several thousand militants have come, could be in really serious trouble. Non-Arab Muslim countries have reason to be watchful too.

There are some fundamental geopolitical realities which may not be palatable to many, particularly to large sections of the Muslims of West Asia, but which will have to be accepted by all in the larger overriding interest of defeating the Islamic State.

It is a huge irony that though much criticised and maligned, whenever a crisis erupts in the Arab world, they ultimately turn to the Americans. The reality is that without them there is no other meaningful way to confront the Islamic State. This war will have to be led by the United States notwithstanding the fact that US policies, along with those of its GCC allies, particularly Saudi Arabia, are primarily responsible for the emergence of the phenomenon of Islamic militancy, and despite the fact that the US has become increasingly unpopular in the "Arab street," the reality is that no other country is capable of, or, equally, if not more importantly, willing to assume that role. Whether anybody likes the US and its policies or not is far less important than these realities; this is also borne out and starkly underscored by the simple fact that until the United States decided upon and initiated airstrikes against Islamic State targets in Iraq that obnoxious entity was expanding rapidly with all opposition speedily crumbling before it. Two months after the proclamation of the

Islamic State regional countries were still engaged in sterile discussions and verbal condemnations of the brutal actions of the Islamic State even as they bickered about who was responsible for its creation and how to meet the challenge it posed.

Another reality is that it is only the United States which can assemble a wide-ranging if not truly global coalition against the Islamic State; such a wide-ranging coalition is absolutely necessary to avoid the inevitable charge that this is another Western war against Muslims. For this reason in particular and because countries of the region must necessarily be seen to be actively involved, it is absolutely essential that Sunni countries must be active participants in actual combat against the Islamic State. It is only the United States which has the clout to get them actually involved because the monarchs are acutely aware that should the war effort fail the first targets of the blowback will be their Sunni regimes. GCC states have long outsourced their security but this time outsiders alone cannot and will not do the job. The US finally cajoled Bahrain, Jordan, Saudi Arabia and the UAE to be actively involved in conducting air strikes in Iraq. For the first time ever Sunni regimes are actual physical participants in a military conflict of their own choice and that too in an alliance with the West against a hugely successful Sunni entity which has the same religious roots as the Saudi Arabia, and has unquestionable appeal to vast swathes of people across the Arab and Muslim world. This is unprecedented. A particularly recalcitrant and prickly Turkey has finally but very reluctantly begun to help by providing transit assistance to Iraqi Kurds to be able to come for the defence of Kobani; and the equally recalcitrant Qatar has also been browbeaten into adopting a more amenable stance. Several Western countries have also been involved in carrying out airstrikes.

Yet another reality is that this war is going to take a long time. This is not a conventional war. Quick results must not be expected. There will be ups and downs. The advance of the Islamic State has already been halted in many sectors and it has been pushed back from some of the territory that it had taken control of. The enemy will increasingly become more fluid and more and more embedded within the civilian population and therefore difficult to tackle without inflicting heavy collateral damage. This is already becoming evident. As the war progresses, the participants and the populations of the participating countries will have to accept paying the price of inevitable higher civilian casualties.

The fighting abilities of local troops will have to be boosted to take on Islamic State fighters on the ground as the war clearly cannot be won from the air and under no circumstances should Western troops in the dozens of thousands be involved. Forces such as the Peshmerga will have to be provided modern arms. US military advisers and even Special Forces are already involved; some increase in their numbers is inevitable—but the saving grace is that they are not and must not in the future be too visible. While troops of Sunni neighbours such as Saudi Arabia and Jordan could become involved later, if necessary, in the Sunni inhabited border regions of Iraq, they must not be involved in Shia or Kurdish regions. The recent killing of four Saudi troops on the Iraqi border could be a precursor to this. It is a particularly good development that the Saudi Embassy is likely to be reopened soon in Baghdad after a gap of 25 years.

It is particularly encouraging that Sunni tribes, Kurds, Shia militias and Iraqi government troops have increasingly been fighting together in several sectors. There are reports that some Sunni tribes are beginning to resist the Islamic State as had happened in Anbar in 2006-7. This is very important because ultimately the war will have to be won primarily by Iraqis in Iraq.

Along with the initiation of American airstrikes, the role of Iranian forces on the ground was a crucial factor in stemming the expansion of IS controlled territory. Iran's known involvement started immediately after Mosul was captured by the Islamic State. Initially Iran's involvement was more or less completely secretive but is increasingly becoming more and more open, publicly acknowledged and expanding beyond the peripheries of the Kurdish region. Control over Mosul Dam could not have been recovered without Iranian help. General Suleimani, the Commander of Iran's Al-Quds Force, has been photographed in various theatres of fighting and has given media interviews, and the recent killing of Iranian Revolutionary Guards Major General Hamid Taghavi in December 2014 in Samarra are high-profile evidence of Iran's very considerable and very effective involvement which is likely to increase even further. Even though there is apparently no direct cooperation between the US and Iran it is tacitly done through the Iraqi authorities and, equally if not more importantly, both sides accept the need for each other's active involvement. In spite of continuing less than friendly public statements, both Saudi Arabia and Iran also recognise that all regional countries would need to be cooperatively involved in the fight against the Islamic State.

Sustaining such disparate and unnatural coalitions fighting the Islamic State is going to be a major challenge. But for the first time each of these otherwise antagonistic countries have a common and particularly dangerous enemy. If this coalition works it could pave the way to dealing with the rising menace of Islamic extremism on the one hand, and the debilitating sectarian divide on the other.

The Islamic State will need to be defeated not only in Iraq but in Syria also. However, the situation in Syria is far more complicated than it is in Iraq. Therefore, the major coalition effort will, for the present, have to be made in Iraq and once substantial gains are made, it will inevitably lead to positive fallout for prosecuting the war in Syria. Meanwhile, the current pace of airstrikes in Syria needs to be enhanced and concentrated help provided in particular sectors such as Kobani, whenever specific situations demand it. Sunni states should not get further involved in Syria.

Defeating the Islamic State is going to be a Herculean task and the war is going to be a long, extremely painful, a rather expensive and particularly bloody process and the world will witness even more violence and brutality than it has already seen in the region. However, if Islamic extremism is to be defeated this is an unavoidable first step. It could also make Arab regimes and their Western patrons finally realise that pandering to religion for short-term geopolitical gains only creates Frankenstein monsters which devour their own creators. The reality is that the leaders of the Arab world have long been in denial about their own responsibility for their problems; the outside world is constantly blamed. The time has come for very serious introspection. The fact is that in the post-World War II era several times more Muslims have been killed by Muslims than by all others put together. As per the Country Threat Index, amongst the ten most dangerous countries in the world, nine are Muslim countries and six are Arab countries. These facts have to be squarely faced. Lasting peace in the Arab world will only be possible if an ideological battle is waged and won within Islam to change the poisonous mindsets that have enveloped much of the Arab world. It is not good enough to say that Islam is a religion of peace and tolerance and that these extremists are fringe elements—the governments and peoples of the Arab world in particular and of the Muslim world in general have to eliminate these extremists and ensure that they will never be given safe haven in their midst in future.

Arab leaders have to recognise that the enormous frustrations of the common people in the Arab world are due to autocratic governance, massive corruption, denial of political space and equal economic opportunities, rampant sectarianism, etc., and that these factors have provided the essential raison d'être for entities like the Islamic State to emerge. Unless there is fundamental socio-political and economic reform, the Arab world will remain mired in instability and violence created by extremism. The reform process must start now, concomitantly with the prosecution of the war against the Islamic State.

Potential Consequences

Some silver linings of the very dark cloud that the Islamic State represents are: First, after the fall of Saddam sectarian and ethnic fissures came to the fore in Iraq in a manner that had never been the case before. Therefore, the involvement of Shias, Sunnis and Kurds in the common fight against the Islamic State is very encouraging and could be cathartic and therapeutic. This bodes well for the future of Iraq since it had begun to appear that its being partitioned along sectarian and ethnic divides was becoming inevitable.

Another positive is that this may finally persuade regional rivals Iran and Saudi Arabia and their respective allies to work together in the common and shared interests of fighting Islamic extremism and sectarianism.

A third, and potentially very important, consequence is that this will ultimately help to promote disenchantment of the average Muslim, particularly of the Gulf region, whether he is Sunni or Shia, with sectarianism and Islamic extremism, and make them realise that these are very dangerous for both.

The fourth is that as the war against the Islamic State progresses well for the coalition it may lead to better possibilities of a negotiated political solution to the civil war in Syria.

The fifth flows from the fact that the intense rivalry between the Islamic State and Al Qaeda for control of the global jihadist movement is already causing intra-jihadist infighting, and this can be expected to escalate throughout the region and augurs well for the defeat of pernicious terrorist groups.

The sixth is that the IS experience has almost certainly triggered the realisation by Arab regimes and their Western patrons that pandering to religion for short-term geopolitical gains only creates Frankenstein monsters that devour their own creators. Some positive indications are already evident in new policy approaches by GCC countries, particularly Saudi Arabia and the UAE, both domestically and otherwise. The march of a million people of all faiths with significant participation of Muslims in Paris on January 11, 2015, after the terrorist attacks of the previous week in Paris, led by 40 world leaders including of Turkey, Jordan, Qatar, the Palestinian Authority, etc., hopefully represents the beginning of a fundamental change of mindsets.

Finally, under President Obama, US policy and actions vis-à-vis West Asia in general and the Gulf region in particular are becoming remarkably different from the utterly disastrous Bush era; the US is now beginning to constructively and cooperatively restore stability in the Gulf region which it did so much to destroy through Bush's unilateral militaristic approach. There can never be stability in the Gulf region without reconciliation between the US and Iran and this is also a clear Obama objective. This ongoing change has very significant immediate, short-term, medium-term and long-term consequences for this region and its immediate neighbourhood. Despite intense domestic criticism of his approach within the US, Obama will strive to continue pushing this approach for the remaining two years of his presidency. In my assessment the legacy of his policy towards the Arab world is likely to be viewed favourably by history.